ABANDONED
IN BERLIN

ABANDONED IN BERLIN

A TRUE STORY

John R. Cammidge

Columbus, Ohio

Abandoned in Berlin: A True Story

Published by Gatekeeper Press
2167 Stringtown Rd, Suite 109
Columbus, OH 43123-2989
www.GatekeeperPress.com

www.johnrcammidge.com

Cover Design by Angelina Valieva

ISBN (hardcover): 9780999855522
ISBN (paperback): 9780999855515
eISBN: 9780999855508

Library of Congress Control Number: 2018954818

Printed in the United States of America

Dedicated to Herta, Vera, and Ellen

Ich werde dich nie vergessen

(I'll never forget you)

Contents

Introduction

ABANDONED IN BERLIN, invites the reader to decide if anti-Semitism in Germany ceased at the end of the Second World War or was concealed by a new set of West German laws. The story reveals the history of a prestigious block of Jewish-owned apartments in Berlin, expropriated under National Socialism at the end of March 1936. The leading characters are a widow and her two teenage daughters, with the story narrated in the third person by Hilda, the only descendant of the youngest child, who currently lives in Novato, Northern California. Researching the family's past begins during June 2016 when Hilda visits Berlin to discover the home where her mother, Ellen, lived as a child and teenager. Through diligent research and the help of people and organizations in Berlin, Britain, the United States, and Israel, a story of persecution, discrimination, courage, and survival emerges.

Important events are exposed, beginning in December 1929, when the father of the family dies suddenly of natural causes. He leaves his wife to bring up his two adolescent daughters and manage the apartment business in the Charlottenburg-Wilmersdorf district of Berlin. The youngest daughter, aged eleven at the time of his death, inherits three eighths of the property, but because she is under age 21 and has no father, is placed under the "care" of a Nazi Guardianship Court. The Court controls all financial decisions affecting the minor, including the property, and slowly uses its power to squeeze the family out of their home, and then out of Germany. Not until the early 1950s can the survivors pursue restitution under newly-created West German regulations. What happens at this time is revealed in *Abandoned in Berlin*.

A Word from Hilda

THE LAST TWO years have been quite an adventure. I never knew how fortunate I was to be alive. All my thanks go to my parents, but especially to my mother, who through her warmth, gave me a happy and caring childhood. It has been like a marathon having people guide and cheer me along the way. It was a race finding the truth about my German ancestry before it was too late. I must thank the author for all his hard work and endless hours of translating, researching, and writing.

Since I can remember, my mother always spoke about her wonderful childhood in Berlin and the beautiful home she grew up in. She told me about the staircase banister she would always slide down, which got her in trouble with her mother. Two years ago, when I was finally able to see that banister, I could imagine my mother as a child laughing as she went down that railing. After we left Berlin, I was visiting the Schoenbrunn Palace in Vienna when it hit me how different my life would have been if Adolph Hitler had not persecuted Jews. I would've led a more prosperous and sophisticated existence.

The more information I found, the angrier I became about what had happened to my family. Ultimately, they were so proud to be United States citizens.

As I come to the conclusion of this story, I am pleased that my family continued with their new life in America and did not let the horrible injustices they experienced under Nazi persecution affect them for the rest of their lives. My mother would always say they had suffered enough for many generations to come.

Hilda

1

Going Away

HILDA STEIN SAT relaxed and cross-legged on the sofa in the front room of her single family townhouse, in Novato, Marin County, California. She stared with satisfaction at the tightly closed, carry-on suitcase, which days earlier, during May 2016, had arrived empty via Federal Express. Now it was stuffed with clothes, European travel books, and personal belongings, ready for a two-week trip to Berlin, Prague and Vienna. The exception was her toiletries. These she was giving to her friend John, who would accompany her. The plan was for John to check in his luggage to simplify the process of passing through airport security.

This was Hilda's first tour with the Rick Steves organization and she was not certain what to expect since the itinerary emphasized walking and mingling with the local community. It would be her second time in Berlin. The first took place during the early 1990s when she traveled with her mother to see her mother's childhood home. Hilda's Austrian-born father did not accompany them; unfortunately he had passed away of natural causes several years earlier. Now in her sixties, Hilda preferred vacationing in faraway places.

Previously, most journeys were to various parts of Northern California, close to where she grew up in San Francisco. Her mother was laid to rest during late 2006 after a long illness, making it easier for Hilda to explore, and freeing her from eldercare responsibilities.

She resigned from a career in banking and now relied on leasing residential real estate as the primary source of income. She was an only child, though she herself had raised two sons and a daughter. They were grown up, living in Sacramento and Oakland, California, and New Jersey. Although Jewish, Hilda's parents always encouraged their daughter not to flaunt her Jewishness. She was happy her friend John would accompany her on the travels. They met during 2010 in a local Starbucks coffee shop, and had grown close. Yet each gave freedom to the other to be self-supporting and remain independent. He was a few years older, and had lost his wife to cancer. He lived nearby, and retired from being a Human Resources executive shortly after they met.

It had taken two days to decide what to pack. If she'd kept count, she probably would hold the world record for the number of times a suitcase could be packed and unpacked during a forty-eight hour period. Her main concern was the weather. It was late May, and in Northern California the climate was already sunny and hot. In Europe, she would experience rain and temperatures well below those she was used to. The flight to Berlin was scheduled for the following afternoon, flying Scandinavian Airlines through Copenhagen to Berlin.

She was excited by the itinerary for this second visit. One of its purposes was to find the five-story apartment building she had been shown by her mother during her first stay. It was where her mother was brought up, and had been owned by her grandparents. The building represented the livelihood of the family prior to the Second World War. From memory, Hilda recalled it as an imposing building, with its floors subdivided into about twenty apartments and several shops located on the ground level. It was situated in the prestigious neighborhood of Charlottenburg-Wilmersdorf in West Berlin.

Standing outside the building many years before, she'd heard about the privileged upbringing of her mother, the servants who looked after the family, and how her mother Ellen, as the youngest child, would spend hours playing with friends in the courtyard. She also talked about sliding down the wooden banister of the building's interior staircase.

Hilda's maternal grandmother was the eldest of six children, and had received a favored upbringing from her father who owned a successful publishing company. Her education was completed at Finishing School in Bonn during the end of the first decade of the twentieth century. This prepared her for Jewish society and marriage to a suitable husband. In turn, she expected her own daughters to develop into refined ladies and marry well.

The youngest daughter was a disappointment as a child, preferring life as a rebel, and enjoying fun with friends, rather than playing with dolls and being concerned with her physical appearance. She spent much of her spare time with the only child belonging to one of her mother's younger sisters. The family lived nearby, and the two girls frequently played together in each other's homes. As the more senior of the two by one year, Ellen believed it was her right to take toys she did not have from her cousin, smuggling them home in her underwear. Consequently, both mothers regularly searched her clothing at the end of each playtime. They agreed a strategy of buying the same playthings for the two daughters, but even this process sometimes failed. There was the occasion when a bicycle was stolen, causing Ellen to ride off on her cousin's bike. Nonetheless, they remained the best of friends during their adult years despite living thousands of miles apart. The independence and self-determination displayed by Ellen during her childhood proved invaluable in helping her cope and outlast German National Socialism.

Hilda was determined to find the home where her mother lived as a child and teenager. Additionally, she wanted to discover details about Berlin during the time of her mother's upbringing, and understand how Jewish life was so forcefully altered by Hitler. Most everything the family possessed was lost during the Nazi years.

Hilda's intention was to use the two days before the organized tour to find the property, and take the Berlin Hop-On, Hop-Off Tour bus to get there. A friend of the family in London gave her the family address. She hoped to recognize the building by the florist's shop on the ground floor that she'd heard about. She hadn't thought about what she'd do once she found the building. It was fair to say Hilda preferred to act without thinking, and deal with the consequences as they arose. But sometimes her impetuousness resulted in pleasant outcomes.

After deciding that the U-Bahn and tram transport systems were too difficult to navigate, she and John each purchased a two-day excursion ticket. While she understood German, she didn't speak it. Growing up, German had been the language at home, but once she attended school, English became her speech of choice. She wanted to discover how many years the property had been family-owned, and what happened during the mid-1930s when it was acquired by someone else.

It was a warm, dry, Friday afternoon, as Hilda and John arrived at the Berlin Tegel Airport. She was annoyed that the airline insisted on her checking her luggage in Copenhagen. The bag arrived on the same conveyor belt as her companion's full-size suitcase. She also worried about petty theft that friends had warned her of in Berlin. She'd heard a story concerning a disappearing suitcase at the airport baggage claim and a snatched purse on the bus to the hotel. For once, she decided a taxi was worth the extra euros. The talkative Turkish cab driver took the opportunity to practice his English and explain the recent transformation of Berlin into a thriving international city. He dropped his two passengers outside their hotel in the former East Berlin, and they checked in for five nights. The hotel was small but comfortable, and made Hilda and John feel welcome. Walking the avenues of East Berlin that evening, Hilda found she understood the Germans who spoke to her, and soon developed a sense of belonging. John spoke French, so was of no help, although he appeared Germanic, and often Hilda would ask the question, and the person would look at John and answer in German.

The streets were alive and vibrant with people sightseeing, shopping, eating, drinking and socializing. The grey, depressing architecture of East Berlin was nearly unnoticeable behind the brightly lit shop fronts, restaurants, and beer gardens. Hilda ate her first Currywurst, a sliced sausage coated with a preparation of curry powder, ketchup, and onions, and presented alongside a portion of French fries. She liked it for the experience, but didn't ask for a second serving.

The next morning Hilda and John returned to the streets of Berlin, mapping their way on foot to the Hop-On, Hop-Off bus stop in Alexanderplatz. They had chosen the Classic Tour which would take them within a mile of her mother's property. From the bus stop, they would need to walk, but the hotel had kindly provided them with a street map of Berlin. The bus traveled slowly, stopping frequently to permit passengers take photos of sites such as Museum Island, the boats on the River Spree, the Brandenburg Gate, the Reichstag, the Victory Column, and the Charlottenburg Palace. This leisurely progress annoyed Hilda and John, who had no intention of taking photographs until their organized tour began. As the bus passed through the upscale shopping district of the Kurfurstendamm, they knew it was time to disembark and walk the remainder of the way to the apartment building. This was a lengthy distance down a residential boulevard, but eventually they found the side street they were looking for. After a brief discussion over direction, they turned right, and a few minutes later Hilda was in front of her mother's former home.

She gasped with astonishment. It was much larger and more magnificent than she remembered, neat and attractive in appearance. She was sure this was the right address because the florist's shop was on the ground floor. The florist greeted Hilda, listened patiently to the family story, and then took her to the back of the store and showed her the building's interior courtyard. Hilda remembered the area from her visit with her mother. She asked if she could go inside the building but was told it was private, and strangers were not allowed. She could have argued, but sensed her host was rigidly disciplined and would stubbornly refuse to allow her to gain access.

Returning to the street, she and John inspected the resident occupant list alongside the front door bells. They had the urge to press any of them but resisted the compulsion. Maybe if they stood there long enough, someone would leave or enter the building. Unfortunately, it was a quiet Saturday, and no resident appeared.

To Hilda, it was irritating and disappointing that she was standing outside the place where her mother grew up, but she was not able to go inside.

She walked over to the jewelry shop on the street corner, and once again asked about entering the building. The reply was the same. Other shops could be visited but it was likely the answer would not change. It was early afternoon and the day continued warm and dry. Hilda crossed the road and turned to stare at the second-floor balcony where she knew her mother spent many summer evenings. She imagined waving at her from across the street. What could she do now? It wasn't time to give up. Hilda was pushy and persistent, and had been taught by her mother to confront challenges and not walk away from difficult situations. Here, however, she needed to find someone willing to help. She would visit every shop. Her idea was to use humility and her innocent looks to persuade someone to assist. John decided to trail behind her, and watch as she prepared to implement the scheme.

2

A Surprise Welcome

THE UNWILLINGNESS TO speak German was the one thing threatening Hilda's plan, if the shopkeepers didn't understand English. She decided to communicate in German, even if it embarrassed her, since at least she could apologize and laugh at her mistakes, and maybe the people would be more obliging if she tried to speak their language. Serendipitously, encouragement came to her as she prepared to cross the road. Two children approached and asked what time it was. Without hesitation, she answered, "fast Mittag." They smiled, thanked her, and quickly disappeared to wherever they were expected. *That wasn't so difficult,* thought Hilda, as the exchange boosted her self-confidence. If children understood her, so might the shopkeepers.

She took one final glance at the property from across the road, observing its steeply pitched black roof, cream walls, and neatly trimmed windows and balconies. It dominated the neighborhood, looking graceful and elegant, and surrounded by other rather ordinary post-war structures. If buildings could speak, what stories this one could tell. She remembered her mother talking about how, during the years of National Socialism, tenants would ask members of the Protective Squad or SS guards (Schutzstaffel) to leave the premises, and shopkeepers would lock their doors to keep out the Hitler Youth. Her grandmother faced enormous risks if something went wrong since not only was she in charge of the building, but she had sole responsibility for the care of Ellen. By all accounts, she spoiled Ellen.

"Who do you think I am?" Hilda's mother would ask years later when entering her daughter's cluttered and disorganized bedroom in San Francisco. "I'm not your dienstmaedchen," she would declare, referring to the housemaid who kept her room neat and organized during her adolescent years in Berlin.

What was clear to Hilda was her mother's fondness for the home in Berlin, and how sad she had been to leave it. Her mother could never remember exactly when she left Germany, but knew it was before Hitler invaded Austria during March 1938. The outcome of leaving had been ten years of refugee status, the first four in Vienna, and the next six in Shanghai. This period of displacement only came to an end during July 1947, when Ellen and her Austrian-born husband, Walter, arrived in San Francisco on the USS General Gordon, having been granted refugee admission by the United States.

In Vienna, Ellen had met the son of the person who looked after the family when they first arrived in Austria. The two fell in love, and once Ellen reached age twenty-one, she married him on November 10, 1939. He was in prison at the time, where he had been confined since around the time of the Vienna Kristallnacht. On November 9 and 10, 1938, paramilitary organizations combined with thousands of civilians to form mobs that torched synagogues, vandalized Jewish businesses, looted and destroyed Jewish stores, and arrested several thousand Jews. A few weeks after he was released, in late 1940, the newlyweds fled to Shanghai.

Hilda's parents arrived penniless in the United States. Her mother found a job as a packer in a shoe polish factory, and her father Walter was employed as a janitor by the Pacific-Union Club. He declared himself a journalist on Hilda's birth certificate in 1950, the profession he followed in Austria, rather than admit he cleaned toilets.

Back in Berlin, Hilda returned across the street to visit the shopkeepers she had not previously spoken with. As she repeatedly explained in German her connection to the building, and ambition to look inside, she encountered a slow and frustrating process. The retailers listened carefully, and on occasion would ask her to repeat herself, but then the reply would be the same, that they could not help. Soon she was entering the last store. It was different from the others in that it sold products only made in Switzerland, and was operated by two non-German men who spoke perfect English, German and French. They had no difficulty understanding Hilda as she returned to speaking her own language. Her story fascinated them and they were shocked that she had never been inside the building.

"Would you like to?" one of them asked. "We have a friend who lives on the second floor and she will be home shortly. We can ask her to show you around. I'm sure she will."

Hilda was astonished by this sudden turn of events. She smiled her acceptance and told the shopkeepers she would wait as long as necessary until the person finished work and returned home. The shopkeepers called their friend who said she would be delighted to show Hilda and John the apartment, and would return in about an hour.

As soon as she arrived, Hilda and John were introduced. The lady was a charming person, easy to talk to, in her mid-forties, an attractive brunette, well-dressed, and a lecturer at a nearby university. She spoke perfect English, with a slight British accent, and lived in the apartment with her young son, who wasn't home on this particular day. She explained that the apartment had been owned by her since the mid-1990s, when she purchased it from a real estate company. She loved the home and was proud to show it to visitors. Most residents, she said, bought their property back in the 1990s, although the landowner kept ownership of the shops. She couldn't remember the company's name and was surprised that the property was once owned by a Jewish family. No one had ever told her.

The three of them entered the building through the side door, and climbed the stone staircase to arrive at her immaculately decorated apartment. The host welcomed her guests inside. She pointed to the Art Deco displays on the ceilings and the molding trim on the doors, telling them that these dated back to when the building was erected. A tour of all rooms was given, ending at the door of a small bathroom, adjacent to the kitchen. This, she said, had been the bedroom of the apartment's dienstmaedchen (servant). She invited Hilda and John to stay for a cup of tea and talked to them about her life as an art student and a single woman. Hilda shared with her stories from her mother.

After the tea was finished, "Let me take you to the top floor attic," the woman volunteered. "It's part of the building only recently repaired, and you can still see the marks of bullet holes made at the time of the war."

The host knew the building suffered additional damage during hostilities, but didn't know the extent. It was some time later, when Hilda was studying correspondence she received from Berlin, that she read how the two apartments above the one she had just visited, were destroyed by incendiary bombs during Spring 1944. The windows of the entire building were blown out by bomb blasts amid the last days of the Battle for Berlin. Additionally, the roof was badly damaged twice, the second time catching fire towards the end of the war. However, compared to many other buildings in the vicinity, the property escaped the fighting relatively undamaged.

The climax of the visit was when the host took her guests downstairs to the main reception area. Still in place was an ornate, polished, wooden banister, curling upwards to the highest floor that Hilda's mother had often talked about. Witnessing it stimulated Hilda's memories. She stroked the wood, saying nothing, but the look on her face and her tear-filled eyes said it all.

With the visit over, the three returned to the store, where more surprises awaited Hilda and John.

As soon as the woman left, the youngest-looking of the two men announced with vigorous enthusiasm, "You need to go here." He gave Hilda a map and a scribbled address that he said was the headquarters of the local District Court, a place he called the Amtsgericht. "These people maintain land registry records for buildings around here.

History on every property is kept, including owners' names, sales dates, and registration documents. You should visit them. Maybe they can tell you when your family owned the building. It's open only a few hours each day, but if you're staying in Berlin until Wednesday, you should have time for a visit."

He continued, "And if you go, please return and tell us the outcome." Then he added, "And we have another idea. You should see the Wir Waren Nachbarn exhibition ("We Were Neighbors"). It's located in the Schoeneberg City Hall, not far from here, and holds records of every person living in this neighborhood who was killed during the Holocaust. The exhibition contains hundreds of biographies and photos, and maybe they can help with your research."

With the information on several scraps of paper, it was time for Hilda and John to say goodbye and start their journey back to the hotel. The day had been exhausting and they were hungry. Before resuming the journey, it was time to eat a late lunch at a delightful Italian trattoria less than a hundred yards away, across the street. They talked about whether they would have time to visit the District Court. Hilda confirmed she had brought her mother's birth certificate and other documents with her, and these might help gain access to the law courts. They decided to delay a decision until after they talked to the tour guide, the following Sunday afternoon.

The Hop-On, Hop-Off buses had finished their daily schedule by the time Hilda and John completed their itinerary of sightseeing, concluding with a walk in the Tiergarten Park. Consequently, there was a five-mile hike back to the hotel, but that didn't seem to matter. Hilda had achieved far more than she expected, and walking through central Berlin on a Saturday evening was a way to soak in the sights and sounds of the city, and reflect on a very successful day. John mapped the way as Hilda chatted about the kindness of the shopkeepers and the tour of the building. After losing their way several times, they finally made it back to the hotel late in the evening. There was no time for dinner. Instead, they retired to the bedroom where they jointly composed a letter that would be presented to the District Court, if they decided to call on it and it wouldn't let them in.

The following morning was devoted to a visit to the remains of the Berlin Wall and a walk through Memorial Park. Somehow the fierceness of the Wall's former purpose was missing because of the presence of so many tourists and commercial activities, despite realistic exhibits of the death zone. The nearby Documentation Center gave a thorough education on the differences between the two Berlins, the Viewing Tower offered a panoramic view of the neighborhood, and the Visitor's Center sold pieces of the Wall as souvenirs. All in all, it was an invigorating walk, but with none of the excitement of the previous day.

Late in the afternoon, it was time for the Rick Steves tour orientation, and introductions to fellow travelers. The group was small, with a range of reasons for people being there. For some, it was curiosity, others an interest in history, and for the musician in the group, to attend a symphony in the Dresden Concert Hall. Hilda and John described their adventures of the previous day and explained Hilda's links to Berlin and Vienna. Afterwards, they sat down with the travel guide for a personal discussion. They were surprised by his interest and encouragement, as he listened to their story. He was a slim, thirty-something, bespectacled German called Carlos, who had led this particular tour many times before. He smiled and seemed eager to help, and he and Hilda discovered they had a number of things in common. Both had one parent born in Germany. Carlos's father had escaped from East Germany to West Berlin during the 1950s, and had met his Costa Rican wife in Bonn. Carlos was proud to be German, and like Hilda, enjoyed the perspective of parents who were able to objectively critique their home country.

Reacting to the unexpected request from his two traveling companions to be let off part of the Berlin itinerary, and using his Rick Steves training, he diplomatically agreed their plan was sensible, but the visit to the District Court should take place on Tuesday rather than Monday. That way they would not miss the important tour of central Berlin he had arranged for Monday morning. He added, during Sunday evening, and before the start of the Monday morning itinerary, he would introduce the group to the Berlin public transport system and instruct them on how to use it. That way Hilda and John would be able to travel by train to the District Court, and he would provide directions to the Amtsgerichtplatz in Charlottenburg, after dinner on Monday evening.

3

The Land Register

HILDA SLEPT SOUNDLY Sunday night, excited that the organized tour was beginning, and she would visit the District Court on Tuesday morning. Carlos had asked her to share the Court experience with the rest of the group during the Prague communal dinner in four nights time.

With her jet-lag beaten, she spent Monday in the company of her colleagues, sightseeing in the heart of Berlin. Thoughts of her mother returned just before lunch, during a visit to the concrete stelae of the Holocaust Memorial, nestled next to the Tiergarten and Brandenburg Gate, and close to the site where Hitler committed suicide. Her mother had lost her home to National Socialism, but at least she had survived the Holocaust. As Hilda sat among the cold, grey, concrete slabs, she felt a sense of achievement for her parents who had defied the horrors of anti-Semitism and established a new life for themselves in America. She recalled her mother's praise for the courage and resilience of her own mother during the harsh years in Berlin under Nazi rule.

Monday evening, Hilda checked her tote bag to make sure it included her passport and birth certificate. She also checked to be certain she had her mother's identification records in case they were needed to gain entry to the District Court. She intended to visit the Land Register where she hoped to inspect the ownership deeds for her family home. The limit of what she knew about the property was her grandparents lived there after they married in 1910, and it was confiscated during 1936.

The couple was told to leave the hotel around nine in the morning and use the U-Bahn to travel the Pankow to Ruhleben line. The train could be boarded at nearby Sansfelderplatz station, and they should get off at Sophie-Charlotte-Platz. Once there, it was only a short walk to the Charlottenburg District Court.

Early Tuesday, dressed in their smartest clothes, Hilda and John left the hotel to make use of the travel instructions given to them by the tour guide. Everything went smoothly and soon they were at their destination. A pair of imposing wooden doors greeted them and then, pushing hard, they found one of the entryways open to reveal a security gate obstructing further access. To the left was a security cage occupied by a solitary guard, protected behind a thick glass window. The female guard came to the see-through barrier and gruffly asked Hilda who she was, why she was there, did she have an appointment, and who was it she wanted to see? This was all in German and Hilda asked the questions to be repeated, more slowly the second time.

Neither Hilda nor John had any idea who they needed to speak with, and Hilda's reply was made more difficult because the guard understood no English. In poorly spoken German, Hilda explained she was trying to trace family ownership of a nearby block of apartments and had been told the Court held land registry records. She'd recently arrived in Germany and did not have time to make an appointment, as she was leaving Berlin for Dresden the following morning.

The guard reacted skeptically, displaying signs suggesting she was suspicious of Hilda's motives. She asked Hilda for her passport and her mother's birth certificate. As these were handed over, Hilda asked the guard to take the letter that had been prepared in case Hilda and John were not allowed into the building. This seemed to unsettle the interrogator, who realized there was something she would have to do if entry was denied. Her attitude softened and she agreed to let them in. The security gate was released, Hilda was given a piece of paper on which a room number was scribbled, and the couple was instructed to go upstairs. The room number turned out to be the location of the General Inquiries office.

A few minutes later Hilda and John were in General Inquiries. A man and woman sat behind a desk monitoring the flow of visitors, but there were none present when the two arrived. Hilda once again used her limited German to explain the reason for the visit, and once more, reactions were discouraging. A barrage of questions was asked that seemed intended to persuade them to go away. The woman receptionist asked to see Hilda's mother's birth certificate and evidence that she was no longer alive. The documents were provided.

Hilda was not a threatening person. She was somewhat petite and had a super-welcoming face that smiled whenever she talked. On this occasion, she nervously tugged at her light brown hair. The people behind the desk reluctantly decided to check their records. Whatever it was they were looking for, they found it. It changed their attitude and they became more cooperative, and the woman wrote down what appeared to be a property registry number, and passed the note to Hilda. Directions were given to visit the Land Register, or Grundbuch as they called it, and the couple was told this department could help them.

The building corridors were long, and the rooms were not clearly numbered, but eventually Hilda and John found the designated office and offered the piece of paper to a man at the desk. He seemed surprised that they had made it so far without an appointment. He took the piece of paper, and as soon as he confirmed the land plot number on the Registry of Deeds, he told his visitors to go next door.

This new room was larger and busier than anything Hilda and John had so far experienced. There was a large reception desk at one end, staffed by several individuals who seemed to be answering questions and passing packages to people who came and went. Along one side of the room was a shelf with a row of desktop computers, several of which were being used. It appeared many people were searching for property records. There were also several rows of chairs in the center of the room, most unoccupied, that were presumably for visitors to sit and wait until they were called to the front desk.

Hilda and John were unsure of what to do next. They sat and looked around. It appeared that clients were either accessing files online, or receiving physical copies at the reception desk. There was a young lady helping who seemed particularly friendly and Hilda took a liking towards her. She became the target of attention. Hilda approached her with a big smile and asked if she spoke English. She didn't. Once more, using her limited German, Hilda explained who she was and why she was there. The woman reacted sympathetically and took away the piece of paper, asking her visitor to return to the chair. A few minutes later she beckoned Hilda back to the counter.

She spoke in German. "I will assist you. We have records and I can access them as soon as I have time. If you leave your address, I'll send copies to your American home, but I need two weeks for research, and the mailing will probably take a similar length of time."

Hilda's persistence once more had been effective. She was delighted by the woman's offer, which seemed genuine. She thanked the assistant and gave her the prepared letter since it included her home address.

People willing to help were always appreciated by Hilda, and on the way out she asked the security guard if there was a florist's shop nearby. She was directed to a store across the street where she bought a bouquet of flowers and a vase to present as a thank-you gift to the helpful woman. On the return, the attendant waived Hilda and John into the building, asking that they deliver the flowers personally. The recipient's reaction indicated she rarely received recognition from her clients.

After a quick lunch, the couple decided to take one final look at the apartment building and let the shopkeepers know what happened at the District Court. They used public transport and quickly found the property. The store owners were pleased to receive an update and congratulated Hilda and John on the results of their visit. They asked to be kept up-to-date by email, and repeated their recommendation that the Wir Waren Nachbarn Exhibition should be visited. It was within walking distance and time was available, so the couple decided to visit.

About forty minutes later, Hilda and John found themselves in a large display hall. It was an awe-inspiring exhibit, but somber and sad. The person in charge listened to Hilda explain her family's history, and went off to research her files. A few minutes later she returned to say that there were no records of Hilda's family, and the property address fell outside the geographic area served by the Exhibition. It was the first disappointment of the tour, but the willingness of the person to help was a welcome consolation.

That evening, the tour guide spoke to the couple to find out what happened during the day. He was pleased the visit was so successful. For Hilda, it was now a matter of wait and see. She trusted the lady at the Land Register and believed she would honor her promise. It was time to resume the tour and prepare for the bus journey to Dresden the following morning.

4

The Vienna Connection

THE TRIP TO Dresden took over three hours on another bright and warm day, and the tour participants arrived at their destination during early afternoon. On the way, the tour guide lectured them on the present-day economy, culture, education, and politics of a unified Germany. After checking in at the Hotel Martha, the tourists walked over the river bridge to observe the reconstruction of a city that was in rubble after the Second World War. They visited such places as the Church of our Lord, the Zinger Palace, Opera House, and the Furstenzug Mural, before everyone was released to spend time on their own.

The following morning, the group departed for Prague, stopping on the way at the fortified town of Terezin that had been converted into a concentration camp during 1941. It seemed to Hilda that wherever she went, she could not avoid the history her parents lived through and survived.

During dinner in Prague, Hilda captivated fellow travelers with her stories from Berlin. They wanted to know more about the family connections with Vienna. She told them her father was born and grew up in the Austrian capital, was imprisoned for about eighteen months during the late 1930s, and after his release from prison, organized an escape to Shanghai for himself and Hilda's mother at the beginning of 1941. It had been a harrowing time for her parents. They were required to visit the Central Office for Jewish Emigration, organized by Adolf Eichmann, to secure exit permits, and received them only weeks before the Nazi government banned all Jewish emigration. Her mother talked about being chased around a table by an expatriation official, but never knew what he wanted.

Hilda told her audience how her grandmother chose Vienna as the place to move to during late 1937, believing it was safer than Berlin and that it would allow her son-in-law to open a bookstore. Although he had a young wife and two infant daughters, there were other members of his family living in Vienna, and they would help take care of the four-year-old and the baby who had just turned one. At first, the family lived comfortably, pawning valuables they brought from their home in Berlin, but after Hitler invaded on March 12, 1938, these resources were quickly exhausted, and the son-in-law was detained in prison for selling illegal books. Anti-Semitism flourished in Vienna once Hitler arrived, as its citizens sought to destroy Jewish prosperity and force Jews to leave the country. The son-in-law's family returned to Berlin with some of its relatives about a year later, leaving him in prison. Hilda's grandmother and mother stayed in Austria.

During October 1938, Hilda's father, Walter, was required to replace his Austrian passport with a German one, printed with a red "J" for Jew on the cover, alongside a swastika and a German eagle. According to Walter's wife, he always refused to wear the yellow Star of David, and escaped to Shanghai before wearing it in public became compulsory.

About the same time in Vienna, Ellen received an invitation from her cousin, Gertrud, who she had played with as a child, offering to sponsor a visa for Ellen to move abroad to Britain. She declined, preferring to wait for her fiancé to be released from prison. As funds ran out, she moved to a Jewish orphanage where she lived and worked. At the same time, her mother was lodged in a care home and forced to scrub the streets of the city. She died penniless, grief-stricken, and broken-hearted on May 1, 1940, the same day that Ellen's husband was released from jail.

Thereafter, Ellen lost contact with her cousin until after the war, when she learned Gertrud was living in London. Gertrud told Ellen that her own mother and an aunt and uncle had been deported during the war from Berlin to the Riga ghetto in Latvia, where they perished.

Hilda's father was imprisoned for eighteen months but always said he was well looked after. The family speculated he received special attention from the guards because his deceased father was a well-known doctor who treated patients who could not afford to pay. During November 1939, prison officials accompanied Walter to City Hall where he married Hilda's mother. Afterwards, Ellen returned to the orphanage and he went back to jail.

The reason why Hilda's father was imprisoned was never announced. Allegedly he tried to smuggle valuables out of the country to help his mother relocate to New York after she remarried. Her new husband had relatives living in America who sponsored their visas. But charges were never filed. Hilda's father was also a Jew and a journalist, both individually good reasons for imprisonment.

"He must have hated his home country?" someone asked.

"No, he didn't," answered Hilda. "In fact, he disappointed my mother by always loving his Austrian heritage. She hated Vienna and never forgave the people there for their treatment of Jews. She said it was a very sad time in her life and she cried a lot."

The conversation by now had turned somber, and the tour guide intervened to redirect the discussion to the topic he had assigned the group during the bus journey from Berlin to Dresden. He paired each person with a "buddy" and asked everyone to discover three things of interest about their partner. Two would be true and one false. Each person was asked to present, and members of the group would try to identify the story that was false. Hilda volunteered herself as a dancer, dog lover, and cosmetics salesperson; the last activity was not true. John put forward bird watching, architect and author, with the middle one made up. It was late in the evening before the quiz was over.

As Hilda returned to her bedroom, a travel colleague asked what had happened to her grandmother's other siblings. "I'm not sure," she replied. "I believe a brother died due to medical conditions, a sister disappeared and turned up in the United States after the war, and the youngest child, a brother, escaped to Shanghai."

A few days later, after an overnight stay in the Czech town of Cesky Krumlov, the tour group arrived in Vienna. As with Berlin, it was Hilda's second visit to the city, the first being with her mother during the early 1990s. She was shown the city but could not remember much about it. She knew from her parents' passports that they left Austria during early February 1941, with travel visas allowing them to pass through Germany, Poland, Lithuania, the Soviet Union, Mongolia, Manchuria, Japan, and curiously, into Santo Domingo, the capital of the Dominican Republic. There was a currency stamp in her father's document permitting him to carry a small amount of German Reichsmark.

Her parents never told Hilda why they ended their journey in Shanghai. Travel papers suggested their ultimate destination was the Dominican Republic. The Asian route was far safer than sailing across the Atlantic with its U-boat risks. Maybe they met people in Shanghai they knew. Whatever their reason, their departure from Austria was just in time. Hilda read about the mass railway deportations from Vienna that began a few days after her parents left the country. Within eighteen months, forty-five thousand Jewish men and women were deported to ghettos, extermination camps, and killing sites. Hilda's mother heard after she left Austria that the children in her orphanage were killed.

Hilda recalled that the most memorable event from her first visit to Vienna was while traveling with her mother on a trolley bus. Several elderly passengers started to scold a group of misbehaving children. Her mother scowled and whispered to Hilda that it was the adults who should be scolded and be ashamed of their treatment of Jews many years earlier.

Hilda enjoyed the sightseeing during the two days in Vienna. With her travel colleagues, she visited the Vienna State Opera House, the Museumsquartier, Belvedere Palace, St. Stephens Cathedral, and Schoenbrunn Palace. At the end of the two days, it was time to say farewell. Her friends wished her success with the investigations, and a Canadian collected everyone's email with the promise to circulate the list after he returned home. Unfortunately, the list never arrived. Hilda booked an extra three nights in the hotel and resumed her family inquiries.

Her first goal was to locate the apartments her father and mother had lived in before they were married. Addresses were on their marriage certificate and she was surprised how easy it was to find them. They were drab buildings with unremarkable architecture. There seemed no point in trying to enter.

The following day, she visited several research organizations to see if she could discover records about her father's family. She had no success. No one seemed interested. It was as if the people she spoke to had forgotten what happened during the Second World War in Vienna, and were not eager to be reminded.

On the final day of the vacation, Hilda and John took the train to Salzburg to hear about another family who had been displaced just before the war, the von Trapp family. The difference was these people had reached the United States, and were given care and protection. It was the best day of Hilda's stay. The scenery was fabulous, the town of Salzburg charming, and the local *Sound of Music* landmarks exhilarating. She even enjoyed the sing-along on the tour bus with the escort dressed in his lederhosen.

But now it was time to return to San Francisco. The sightseeing had been enjoyable, celebrating her birthday at the Vienna Opera was memorable, and discovering the winery on the outskirts of Vienna that she thought her mother took her to visit many years earlier was unforgettable. She was disappointed the Austrian people generally acted aloof, and appeared uncaring and unwilling to admit their country's involvement in National Socialism. To them, it apparently never happened. They were "occupied" by the Germans, and like many other parts of Europe, claimed they were not guilty of anti-Semitism.

By contrast, the Berliners acknowledged the actions of their ancestors and consistently tried to be helpful. Her confidence speaking German had improved, she had learned how to prepare the wiener schnitzel that her mother cooked for her, and she created several new friendships among the tour group. Most importantly, she was confident that the lady at the Charlottenburg Land Register would deliver on her promise. She would be patient; it was only two weeks since the visit to the District Court, and soon she would learn about the years her family owned the property that she had gazed at in Berlin.

5

Early Revelations

S EVERAL WEEKS LATER, back in Novato, California, Hilda
was increasingly apprehensive about whether or not the woman
in the Land Register would fulfill her commitment. Six weeks
had passed, and the lady promised a reply within four. An irritated
Hilda was drafting a letter to remind the woman of her pledge when
the package arrived. It was a large, bulky envelope containing several
official-looking documents. Everything was in German and Hilda
understood none of it. Her neighbor, who read and spoke German,
took charge of the cover letter, while a doctor friend called Bill,
living in nearby Larkspur, agreed to translate the legal contracts.
The remaining pages were converted into English by Hilda using her
computer. She anxiously hoped that the correspondence would reveal
details about her family's ownership and describe the circumstances
under which the building was lost during 1936. The letter confirmed
the address of the building she visited as Guntzelstrasse 44, at the
corner of Holsteinische Strasse 19.

The cover letter was signed by the woman Hilda talked to in
the District Court and was quickly translated by the neighbor. It
explained that the materials in the Register of Deeds confirmed
Hilda's family owned the property from 1919 to 1936. It showed
her grandfather taking possession during June 1919, but unfortunately the handwritten document describing the transaction was

written in a German script known as "sutterlin" and was impossible to read.

Maybe that didn't matter. The 1919 purchase price was expressed in German Papiermarks, a currency discontinued in late 1923 because of German hyperinflation following the First World War. When the property was registered, there were thirty-three Papiermarks to the United States dollar, but four years later, the German currency was worthless. One trillion marks equaled a single dollar and a new currency had to be introduced a year later, with an exchange rate of one billion Papiermarks to one Reichsmark. The importance of the document was to confirm the date of family ownership rather than to discover the property's value at the time.

Hilda now knew the apartment building she visited in Berlin was her ancestral home, and had been the family source of income for seventeen years. Other correspondence among the papers she received implied her grandparents might have occupied the property for a longer period of time. There was evidence they lived at the same address as early as 1908, not long after the property was constructed. Hilda's interpretation was the family must have been well-off and possessed the resources to give both their daughters untroubled and carefree lives.

There were two additional ownership deeds, one dated 1933 and the other 1936. Each was lengthy, and Hilda waited for Bill to complete his translations. The November 1933 document included a copy of her grandfather's death certificate. She learned he died during December 1929, and his two daughters and wife inherited the building in accordance with German inheritance law.

German estate regulations required property to pass to next-of-kin immediately after death, with proportionate shares compulsorily assigned. Hilda's grandmother received a quarter ownership and her grandmother's two daughters each inherited three-eighths. In effect, Hilda's mother, as an eleven-year-old, suddenly became the heir to a significant portion of the family business. The arrangement was certified in a 1933 ownership document, and the value of the building was recorded as 150,000 Reichsmark (U.S. $60,000). It was unclear whether the appraisal was at the date of death or on the day of certification. As a result, each daughter owned property worth 56,250 Reichsmark (U.S. $22,500), or an estimated half million dollars in today's value.

The third deed, dated March 31, 1936, was the most alarming. It recorded the conveyancing of the property to a new owner. The person's name was given and he carried the prefix of Hauptmann or Captain. It was unclear if the title referred to his status in the military or simply acknowledged him as the "head man" of his family. A more disturbing aspect was that the building had been declared "Aufgelassen" or "Abandoned" in the Registry of Deeds. Hilda wondered what this meant. There was no explanation. She speculated it was possible her family had been forced out of their home by anti-Semitism, and the property confiscated. As she solved one mystery, others seemed to emerge. There were no signatures on the last document, leaving Hilda to wonder if the transaction had been voluntary.

The same document showed the sale price for the property was 208,000 Reichsmark (U.S. $84,000), but the financial arrangements were complex and unusual. A 90,000 Reichsmark (U.S. $36,000) mortgage apparently existed that was assumed by the purchaser. Hilda always understood the family owned the property outright and did not need to borrow money. There was no explanation of why, when, and how this loan had been obtained. Another 78,000 Reichsmark (U.S. $31,500) was to be paid to Hilda's grandmother and two daughters, presumably immediately, although there was nothing in the documents to confirm it was actually paid.

The biggest surprise was the third component. An amount of 40,000 Reichsmark (U.S. $16,000) was set aside to be paid as a delayed purchase mortgage. This meant the purchaser was not required to release the funds until, at the earliest, April 1941. During the five-year deferral period, quarterly interest payments were due at an annual interest rate of five percent. This seemed a strange arrangement, especially if the family was considering leaving Germany at the time of the sale. Before the due date for this payment, war would have begun,

Hilda's grandmother had died, and Hilda's mother and father fled to Shanghai. It was incomprehensible that the family would accept such an arrangement. Maybe they had no choice. Was the money ever paid or did it remain an outstanding debt? Did the family of the 1936 purchaser still own the property? Were there bank records that would show payments had been made?

It seemed a series of new questions had arisen and the task Hilda set for herself was now much more complex. It was difficult to decide what to do next. If the research was continued, she might unearth family secrets that were embarrassing or shocking. She talked to John and other friends, and they told her she should continue. Maybe she would discover details of the purchaser, establish the chronology of ownership after 1936, and possibly investigate if proceeds from the sale were actually received by her family.

She wrote to her cousin in London to tell her what she had begun and heard back that the cousin's mother often spoke of the 1936 purchaser as a person strongly disliked by the family. Hilda's aunt had passed away in 1992.

Eventually, Hilda decided she was not going to give up. She would investigate the background of the 1936 purchaser, write to the lady in the Land Register requesting ownership records after 1936, and see what more she could learn about the circumstances of the sale.

6

An Olympic Year

ILDA AND JOHN sat in front of their computers for hours trying to find information on the internet. It was a frustrating and unproductive process. The starting point was discovering details about the Hauptmann or Captain who had bought the building since from his title, they thought he might have fought during the war. They were out of luck. People with the same last name surfaced, but everything was circumstantial, without proof that any individual was the person Hilda and John were looking for.

A captain of the same name was found to be a member of the Luftwaffe, but was killed in action during the war. Hilda's ambition was to discover an address that would allow her to contact the buyer's successors. She had not thought through the wisdom of the idea and the range of consequences it could provoke.

She also wanted to understand why the building was declared "abandoned." The term was supposed to apply to property where possession had been relinquished and the owner left the premises with no intention of returning. But why would Hilda's family sacrifice their home and business in this way after so many years of ownership? It was difficult to imagine them doing this voluntarily. Maybe the Nazi government seized the building and handed it over to the German?

Persecution of Jews and confiscation of property was normal

during this period of National Socialism. Hilda researched events in Berlin during 1936 and was surprised to learn the first few months of the year were a period of relative calm, as German authorities sought to conceal discrimination so that anti-Semitism didn't interfere with preparations for the August 1936 Berlin Olympics. Under these circumstances, the classification of "abandoned" might simply mean the owners had decided to leave Germany, or that the property was in poor physical condition.

The other consideration was whether the sale price was fair. Hilda calculated it was thirty-eight percent higher than the valuation given in the 1933 document, but she didn't know the effective date of that appraisal or if the property was intentionally undervalued for inheritance tax purposes.

Her most important issue was whether the family had received proceeds from the sale, and in particular, if the deferred mortgage and quarterly interest payments had been disbursed. She thought it important to track down the family's 1930s bank accounts to see what was received. She wondered if the Land Register kept these records. Another letter could be sent, and at the same time, she could ask about ownership of the property from 1936 to the present day. Her mother always said the family could not take money out of Germany, and therefore it was possible the funds were left behind and had been appropriated by the banks.

She worried she might abuse the cooperation of her friend by requesting too much information. A personal injury attorney called Jack, living in Mill Valley a few miles away, advised her she had every right to request ownership records, including financial documentation; after all, it was a Court and that's what these institutions were supposed to do. She prepared and mailed her request.

Hilda's mother had spoken about her first visit to Germany after the war. The mayor of Berlin invited refugees to spend a week in the city as his guest. They were given accommodations, spending money, theater tickets, and reimbursed for their travel expenses. Hilda's mother visited her former home and was amazed to see it in near perfect condition. She told Hilda standing in front of the building was a weird sensation. Memories of a cheerful past in Berlin flooded back, but she had no interest in returning to Germany having settled into a safe and happy life in America.

Hilda also received recommendations to contact the German Consulate in San Francisco and to investigate her legal rights. The latter prompted her to correspond with an Israeli law firm specializing in Nazi-seized property. The firm replied almost immediately, telling her that claims in West Germany were finalized during the 1960s and no new demands could be submitted. She was disappointed, but not discouraged, since her research was motivated by curiosity, not financial gain. She contacted the German Consulate to explain what she was doing and to ask if someone could offer her guidance on what she should do next, including whether or not she might be able to trace financial records from the 1930s. A meeting was arranged for November 14, 2016.

Hilda found it hard to believe that a brief visit to Berlin could generate such a complex investigation. Everyone she spoke to seemed interested in her story and wanted to hear more. She sent an email to the Berlin shopkeepers telling them what was going on, and they replied, giving her more encouragement. They promised to pass on the progress report to the apartment owner. Hilda had no idea what she would discover next, and patiently waited to hear back from the Charlottenburg Land Register.

7

The Fall of the Wall

THE NOVEMBER 14, 2016 meeting at the German Consulate was no sooner confirmed than additional materials arrived from the Land Register. Hilda's contact replied within a day of receipt, and once more, everything was communicated in German. Her Berlin colleague provided a chronology of ownership, what she called Erste Abteilung, from 1936 until present day. Regulations prevented her from sharing the detail of property registrations that did not involve Hilda's family.

The translated letter conveyed the discouraging news that the office was not responsible for financial documents. "The implementation of arrangements which closed the contract in 1936 is a matter for the parties to it, and is not monitored or checked by the Register office," the letter stated.

Hilda was disappointed and uncertain what else she could do to find the bank records. Maybe the German Consulate would help. Alternatively, she might write to German banks, but she had no idea which ones. It was predictable and probable that her grandmother kept cash in the house rather than in a bank because of the hostile political situation, and if so, no bank account would be traceable. She thought she was coming to an end, at least for this aspect of her investigations.

The chronology showed the captain and his family owned

the property from 1936 to 1990. Once the purchaser's name was registered, there were no sales transfers for the next fifty-four years. Records were kept by the Schoeneberg District Court, rather than Charlottenburg, indicating the buyer probably did not live in the apartments. Schoeneberg was the place Hilda and John visited during their trip to Berlin, the location of the Wir Waren Nachbarn Exhibition.

There was no new ownership recorded after the war, and no indication that Hilda's family sought restitution for the building. Her parents never talked about reparations, only that the property was permanently expropriated in 1936.

Until 1990, the property was registered twice to the same family. The first occasion was in September 1974, when the title was conveyed to a woman with the same surname. A will was filed on October 21, 1965, and Hilda and John reasoned the original purchaser must have died that year. The inheritor was born during December 1895, and might be a sister, a mother, or a wife.

There was also an earlier unusual note added to the files. A few days after the 1936 purchase, the buyer asked the District Court to pay a widow, who shared his last name, a yearly maintenance pension of 3,600 Reichsmark (U.S. $1,500), with payments to be made quarterly, commencing July 1936. Her earlier maiden name was distinct, suggesting she might have been the purchaser's mother, and possibly her husband had recently died. From this Hilda deduced the inheritor might have been the owner's sister, and the 1936 purchase was possibly funded by a legacy inherited by the buyer from his deceased father.

The second transfer occurred on March 20, 1981, when a Certificate of Inheritance was filed with the Schoeneberg Court, naming several people as co-owners. The Land Register changed the ownership records several years later on August 11, 1988. There was no explanation for the delay. The list of new owners gave Hilda and John renewed hope. Maybe they could now trace one of these names and discover the whereabouts of the family, but unfortunately, once more, nothing specific was found. Many Berliners shared the same last name and none had the right combination of first and last designations.

The chronology gave details of more recent ownership. Possibly by coincidence on November 9, 1989, the day after the Berlin Wall came down, a Swiss businessman initiated negotiations to purchase the building. No details were provided except that the transaction was completed during March 1990.

Two years later, the businessman sold the apartments to a privately-owned, Berlin-based, real estate company. The Land Register listed the new owner as Onnasch Baubetreuung GmbH and Co., based in Berlin; occupying headquarters just south of the Tiergarten. Conveyancing took place on March 25, 1992. This time, checking the internet, Hilda and John found details to the firm. It was a limited partnership, founded in 1961, and there was reference to its current forty-member Berlin staff and their administration of approximately three thousand residential units. The company's mission was acquiring, converting, and managing properties.

The next step for Hilda seemed to be to contact the real estate developer, although she didn't have much information to communicate. Possibly the firm held more details about the 1936 sale, although its acquisition occurred over fifty years after her family gave up ownership of the building. She had nothing to offer that would incentivize the firm to exchange particulars, and the company might not have conducted due diligence back to 1936. If the outcome of the communication was no more than an acknowledgement, nothing would have been achieved. Hilda thought maybe she needed more facts before communicating with the company.

She asked several United States-based Jewish organizations for advice. They were sympathetic to her difficulties, but not helpful with direction, leaving it up to her to decide what to do. Obstacles to progress increased and Hilda once more considered ending her efforts. John encouraged her not to, and suggested she delay a decision until after the visit to the German Consulate. She had already invested a great deal of time and it was likely this would be her last opportunity to learn about her German ancestry. The chance of a breakthrough was probably slight, but if all else failed, there was still the real estate firm to contact. Hilda accepted the suggestion and turned her attention to preparing for the meeting with the German Consulate. John would accompany her and accepted the task of assembling a binder containing copies of all the documents sent by the Land Register, and would add birth, marriage, and death certificates for Hilda's parents. Five months had passed since the vacation in Berlin, and Hilda was struggling to continue with her research. Maybe the German Consulate could help.

8

The German Consulate

IT WAS A warm, sunny November morning, as Hilda drove across the Golden Gate Bridge towards the German Consulate. The California sun had risen in a clear, pale-blue sky and reflected off the white skyline of the City across the Bay. The weather conditions strengthened Hilda's confidence that the day would be successful. Her leather and fabric tote bag lay on the back seat, holding everything she thought she would need: her passport and birth certificate, a binder containing the materials she received from the Land Register, her parents' registration documents, and a pen and paper to take notes. John sat in the passenger seat as the journey was completed without mishap. Today's events would decide whether or not Hilda would continue her investigation.

A new piece of information she and John had recently found was that the German currency used in the 1936 sale, the Reichsmark, was replaced in June 1948 by the Deutsche Mark. The exchange rate applied was approximately one Deutsche Mark to ten Reichsmark, which represented an enormous devaluation of the former currency. If Hilda's family kept money in a German bank account, it would be close to worthless after the Second World War, having lost ninety percent of its value. By contrast, the family property would retain most of its financial worth, as presumably it continued to be rented. It was easy to imagine the buyer resisting attempts to reclaim the building once the war was ended since he would lose nine-tenths of his original investment. Reichsmark would be converted to Deutsche Marks to calculate the repayment Hilda's family would need to make to compensate him for the return of the building. Banks similarly would lose large amounts if their Reichsmark-denominated mortgages were cancelled.

Hilda read how properties were sometimes returned to their prior owners during the early 1950s, often because damage caused by the fighting made them uninhabitable. Restitution laws were put in place by West Germany to control the process of return. Situations occurred where claimants and defendants negotiated monetary settlements, permitting the purchaser to keep the property, and to compensate the original owner with a cash settlement. There were also examples of coldhearted Germans who campaigned strongly to keep their property, arguing it was purchased legally and at a fair price. She wondered how her family might have been treated if they had submitted a claim. So far, there was no evidence that the family sought restitution, and the materials from the Land Register implied either one was not submitted, or if it was, it was unsuccessful.

During the journey, Hilda told John she thought she wanted to continue the research. She felt she needed to know if her parents received justice for the misery and hardship suffered under National Socialism. The intention was not to pursue legal channels but simply to know the truth about the treatment of her parents. John promised he would help. The two of them would work together to identify future steps, draft correspondence to support inquiries, translate documents from German to English, and organize materials to improve continuity and comprehensiveness.

On arrival at Pacific Heights, Hilda found parking less than a block away from the Consulate. She inserted the maximum parking fee in the meter, gathered her tote bag, and the two of them walked the half block to two connected orange, brick-built townhouses that were the official residence of the German consular office. Access to the building was blocked by a tall, ornate iron gate with a button to press to gain access. The English-speaking guard from the security lodge walked over to greet them. After opening the gateway, the guard checked their identities, inspected the contents of Hilda's bag, performed body searches, and checked paperwork to confirm an appointment existed. When he finished, he pointed to the passport office and instructed them to enter.

The dim illumination within the building contrasted with the bright orange light reflected off the brickwork exterior. The interior dullness was due to the dark wooden-paneled walls, small windows, and low lighting. Hilda first explained to the receptionist that she wasn't there to apply for a German passport, but instead hoped to talk to a representative from the Consular and Legal Affairs department about a German property that formerly belonged to her family. The person reacted cautiously, asking Hilda why she thought the Consulate could help. Hilda explained her contact with the Charlottenburg Land Register, and the assistant eventually was persuaded the inquiry was genuine. She phoned someone who Hilda assumed was in the appropriate department. The person at the other end of the line agreed to a meeting. "The person you want to see is not here on a Monday. It's her day off. However her deputy is willing to talk to you," Hilda was told.

Hilda and John were asked to go next door and wait in a conference room. The new room was similarly dark, but much larger, with most of its space occupied by a large conference table placed in the center of the room. There were several clusters of people randomly situated around the table, and each appeared to be receiving help from a Consular official. After a few minutes, a tall, slim, clean-shaven, and well-dressed gentleman arrived. He was fair skinned, blue eyed, with darkish colored hair, and a prominent nose. He clearly understood English but spoke with a strong German accent. He seemed eager to assist but confessed he had only recently taken over his current position. He sat down and asked the couple the reason for the visit.

Hilda explained, showed him the binder, and apologized for bothering him. Despite moments of perplexity, he seemed to find the story captivating. He asked a few questions, but wasn't sure how he could help. It was an unusual inquiry, he stated, not one the Consulate normally dealt with. Hilda asked him if he thought she was wasting her time. He thought not.

He was surprised that the District Court in Charlottenburg had told her it could not provide financial information. His understanding was that the Courts held all forms of personal records for citizens living in the local community, and German standards were to archive information for at least a hundred years. He suggested Hilda reach out to the office once more, and expressed pride in Germany's method of maintaining records. Contact with the real estate company was also recommended, but the use of legal representation was unnecessary, he suggested.

He declined to accept the binder and, as he closed the meeting, wished Hilda and John success, excused himself and left. At 10.45 in the morning, the meeting was over. It was time for an early lunch. Hilda was pleased with the outcome and told John she would continue her investigations. Once they had eaten, they returned to Novato to draft a third letter to the woman at the Land Register.

First, however, Hilda wanted to thank the Consulate person. She drafted an email and copied his boss, the head of Consular Affairs, and promised to act on his advice. Nothing further was heard from the government office. Another note was sent to Hilda's cousin in London describing the meeting and telling her that she and John would try and trace what happened to the 1936 sales proceeds. John helped draft a third letter to the Land Register in which Hilda repeated her request for financial records. She asked, if none were available, were there other places she could turn to for this type of information?

The letter was mailed and Hilda waited to hear back from Berlin. She hoped the next stage of research would be more productive and she would learn new details about the sale of her grandmother's home. For now, she would not contact the real estate company.

9

Troublesome Answers

U NFORTUNATELY, THE THIRD round of inquiries was not very successful. Once again, the Land Register replied that it was not in charge of financial records and did not know if German banks kept account histories. The response was contrary to what Hilda expected in light of the advice from the German Consulate. What she overlooked was the consular official was referring to District Court responsibilities, whereas Hilda's contact dealt only with documentation maintained by the Land Register. The importance of this distinction would become evident later.

Hilda trusted her Berlin friend. She was always timely and clear with her replies, and gave whatever help she could. This answer was no exception. At the end of the letter, there were contact details for two organizations, the Jewish Community of Berlin (Centrum Judaicum), and the Berlin-based Federal Association of German Banks (Bundesverband deutscher Banken), that her friend suggested might hold relevant files. The Jewish Community archived the history of Jews in Berlin, and the Federal Association of German Banks represented the German private banking industry and could retrieve its members' banking records. Contact addresses were provided and Hilda quickly dispatched letters to these institutions, plus a thank you note to her Land Register helper.

Several months later, she was still waiting for replies from both organizations and began to lose hope that she would ever hear from either of them. Follow-up correspondence went unanswered. The Jewish Community of Berlin appeared exclusively committed to managing the Berlin Synagogue and arranging Exhibitions of Jewish Life, and Hilda decided to eliminate further contact. The Association of German Banks seemed to ignore her stubborn correspondence and then, just as she was preparing to concede defeat, a reply arrived in mid-July 2017. It was from the Association's Legal Affairs department and politely explained the organization was unable to launch a search for family records. It referred to what it called "war-induced chaos" during the years up to 1945, and argued a hunt for account balances would be complex and likely unsuccessful. Even if data could be traced, amounts would be denominated in Reichsmark, a currency no longer in use.

But the Association provided a glimmer of hope. The representative suggested that if her relatives fled Germany due to persecution of the Jews, Hilda should contact the German Federal Office for Central Services and Unresolved Property. If property had been confiscated, a claim might still be possible and the Federal Office would know. Hilda acted quickly and submitted an inquiry.

While waiting for the response, she returned to the internet to investigate law firms involved in restitution claims. In a number of cases, their success left a lot to be desired. She read about the sixty-thousand Jews whose requests for special pensions due to subsistence wages during the Second World War were turned down, and how owners of stolen paintings and sculptures encountered delays and the reluctance of German museums to return Nazi-looted art.

She found a nearby law firm whose website said it specialized in Jewish property restitution. Contact was made to see if it could help. The person receiving the inquiry said he was willing to search for bank accounts, but for a fee, and also offered, if it would be helpful, to search for information on whether or not Hilda's family applied for restitution after the war. He was not optimistic about the outcome and confirmed what Hilda already knew, that it was too late to apply for compensation. Hilda, who was known for her thriftiness, decided to continue working on the investigation alone.

She sent letters to several Holocaust organizations such as the Conference on Jewish Material Claims against Germany, and the International Center for Holocaust Reparations. Once again, she was told there was no program available for filing new claims. Action against governments and public entities might be possible, but private individuals could no longer be prosecuted. The impression was that there were still many organizations involved in the consequences of anti-Semitism, but no one seemed interested in Hilda's specific situation. She would have to proceed alone.

The cousin in London conveyed her expectations that the research would never produce meaningful results. It had been seventy-two years since the war ended, and there were very few witnesses to remember what happened. John encouraged Hilda to persevere and be tolerant of delays. After all, it had only been a year since the research began. Hilda wasn't sure, but since John was doing most of the work, she accepted his advice.

It was at this point she found a box of family photographs and correspondence stored away in her garage. The collection had been placed there after her mother died, but she had never checked its contents. It turned out to contain photos of German relatives, some scenic pictures of the Alps, and a photograph of the family's apartment building taken several decades earlier. She could make out some of the store names on the ground floor and it was winter because snow was on the street. There was also correspondence dating from 1953 to 1954, between her parents and her aunt and uncle in London, and several exchanges with lawyers. Everything was typed in German and it would take a considerable time to translate, but the impression was something had happened at that time. As Hilda began to complete the translations, her intuition proved correct. She read correspondence that her mother and aunt were discussing restitution claims and had begun legal action to recover ownership of the property. This surprise discovery stimulated Hilda and John into more vigorous efforts. There was still the expectation that the Central Services office in

Berlin would reply and Hilda could use that information, and more internet research, to fill in the blanks and complete the story.

She and John investigated the emigration of German Jews that took place during National Socialism. Thirty-seven thousand Jews departed in 1933, Hitler's first year of authority. They were principally professionals, writers, academics, and politically-active members of society who were affected by the dissolution of political parties, the abolition of trade unions, and the loss of employment. Most lost their jobs as a result of the April 1933 Nazi law known as "The Restitution of the Professional Civil Service." This authorized public institutions in Germany to dismiss civil servants considered "untrustworthy." Jewish teachers in public schools and universities, Jews working in government, and Jewish lawyers, notaries, and doctors were all impacted, and concurrently Jewish-owned businesses became the target for either closure or transfer of ownership to Aryans.

Hilda recalled stories from her mother about attending school and how education became chaotic during her teenage years in the mid-1930s. She mentioned attending a Catholic school that expelled her. She was bullied, friends stopped talking to her, she was called a Jewish Pig (Judenschwein), and forced to attend race-knowledge classes that told her about the untrustworthy, short, stocky Jews with dark eyes and crooked noses. Some of her teachers wore Nazi-style uniforms. She refused to stand in class and give the Hitler salute, and it was this disobedience that caused her removal from school.

Her mother transferred her to a nearby all-Jewish institution attended by pupils from the local community, who generally came from relatively well-off German-Jewish middle and upper-middle class backgrounds. Instructions were similar to the Catholic school except Hebrew classes were included, and language courses in French and English offered.

The other story Hilda recalled was how her mother had lost contact with her sister before the war, and only learned after she arrived in the United States that her sibling had moved to England during 1939. She traced her sister's family to a small town about fifty miles northwest of London.

Although Hilda was never close to her English relatives, she knew the Polish uncle helped the British during the Second World War, and she decided to investigate what happened to him and his family. Apparently, Hilda's aunt, after returning to Berlin from Vienna, arranged for her eldest daughter to move to England after the "Night of Broken Glass" ("Kristallnacht"). This took place in Berlin on November 9, 1938, when Jewish businesses were trashed and looted, synagogues and Jewish-owned buildings set on fire, many Jews murdered, and thirty thousand dragged off to concentration camps. As a result, the British introduced a scheme called "Kindertransport" ("Children's Transport"), to allow infants and children up to the age of seventeen to move to the United Kingdom without their parents. The transfer was anticipated to be temporary. Around ten thousand arrived during the period December 2, 1938 to September 1, 1939, the day the Second World War began. The eldest daughter was placed with a guardian family in Edgware, London, who took good care of her.

Two months later, Hilda's aunt secured permission for herself to move to Britain with her younger child, now aged nearly two, and was placed in the home of a Jewish family in north London. It was an unpleasant experience. Employed as a maid, she was not granted time off, was not paid for her services, had to sleep in the same bed as her daughter and the child of the couple who employed her, and was locked in the house when the family went out. Eventually she escaped, and was taken care of by a local Jewish organization that gave her enough money to rent a room.

She spent the next several weeks seeking approval for her husband to join her from Poland. Apparently he had returned to his home country in late 1938 when Germany cancelled residency permits for all foreign-born Jews, including Polish people. Poland had responded by announcing it would not accept the return of Jews of Polish descent after the end of October 1938, and consequently Germany expelled twelve thousand Polish nationals before that date. Fortunately, Hilda's aunt was successful, and her husband arrived in Britain two days before the Second World War began.

He was first sent to a refugee camp in Kent, and from there enlisted in the British Army, where he became a cook. He served in France, and after Dunkirk, shifted between various military installations across Britain, ending up posted just north of London in Bedfordshire. His wife placed her youngest daughter in an orphanage in the county of Kent and retrieved the eldest child from the adopted family. She found work in Boots, a chain of chemist stores, as a shop assistant until her husband was able to open his own business after the war was over. He used the thirty pounds sterling and the suit he was given when released from the military to buy army surplus and sell it in local market places. At about the same time, he took home his youngest daughter from the Kent orphanage where she had spent the last five years.

Hilda wondered who had suffered the most as a consequence of German anti-Semitism, her parents in Shanghai or her aunt and family in Britain. Her relatives arrived in Britain, by all accounts, penniless. The Nazis apparently approved a shipment from Berlin for Hilda's aunt, to include a few personal belongings, but they were lost in transit.

Hilda and John continued to translate the correspondence found in the garage and looked forward to an early reply from the Central Services Office in Berlin. Hopefully they were making progress, but they weren't sure.

10

Disclosure

I T SEEMED LIKE forever, but the reply arrived after two weeks, at the end of July 2017, from the Library of the Federal Office for Central Services. It was a major breakthrough. The author had researched the institution's records and found correspondence dated June 12, 1953, referring to a restitution process involving Guntzelstrasse 44, the former home of Hilda's family. The letter was from the Property Finance department in the Wilmersdorf District of Berlin, notifying the Berlin City Senator for Finance, Special Property, and Construction that a reimbursement request had been filed against the 1936 purchaser by a group called the Jewish Restitution Successor Organization. The Wilmersdorf District was incorporated into the Charlottenburg borough many years later as part of administrative reforms in Berlin. The writer from the Federal Office recommended Hilda contact the Berlin State Archives (Landesarchiv Berlin) because it appeared to hold the legal papers.

This was wonderful news and signaled the possibility that Hilda and Johns' research would accomplish a successful outcome. It was learned the attributed letter referred to a claim sent to the Berlin Restitution Office on March 26, 1953, informing the agency that the Jewish Restitution Successor Organization was requesting the return of the property, claiming it was forcibly acquired on March 31, 1936, as a result of National Socialism. The buyer objected to the request, arguing the sellers were fortunate enough to be still alive, and in 1936 waived their rights to own the building. This was the first conclusive correspondence received by Hilda that confirmed a restitution claim was submitted. She now hoped the information from the State Archives, combined with her own garage materials, would explain the sale and describe what happened after the war.

Checking the internet, John discovered the Berlin State Archives held records for the complete history of the City, including the borough of Charlottenburg-Wilmersdorf, and its District Court handled this particular claim. Hilda contacted the Berlin State Archives, and in a matter of days, received more good news. Not only did the repository hold documents, but the dossier amounted to more than three hundred pages, and the office was willing to scan and send a copy to Hilda. It apologized that the project would take several weeks because of its size and the availability of personnel resources. She was also warned everything was in German. The repository was told to proceed, with the understanding it would take three months to copy and mail everything to Hilda.

As they waited, Hilda and John researched the German restitution process of the early 1950s to understand the legal conditions under which claims were adjudicated. They also wanted to complete the translation of the remainder of the garage correspondence.

Their first discovery was that the Jewish Restitution Successor Organization was set up in 1948 to handle property restitution claims in the American-occupied zone of Germany, but that Hilda's family home was located in Berlin's British sector. Therefore, the restitution responsibility belonged to the British Jewish Trust Corporation. However, this Hamburg-based agency used the Berlin office of the Jewish Restitution Successor Organization to institute legal proceedings in West Berlin. This was a complexity unanticipated by Hilda.

When created in 1950, the first task of the Jewish Trust Corporation was to identify properties confiscated under National Socialism in all British territories. Displaced persons were asked to register lost property and German owners were expected to declare their purchases. That didn't happen, and eventually seventy percent of the

Trust's claims resulted from its own investigations. In August 1950, it was given access to files, records, and registers kept by German courts, land registries, banks, public notaries, and other authorities.

It appeared this was how Hilda's family home was identified, and not because of a specific claim from her relatives. The whereabouts of Hilda's mother, sister, and grandmother at the time were unknown, and a demand was filed on their behalf. German restitution law defined the procedures for the return of confiscated property, and if a settlement could not be reached between the parties, District Restitution Chambers were appointed to adjudicate claims. In Berlin, these judgments could be appealed to the Berlin Court of Appeals, and thereafter, to the Supreme Restitution Court of West Berlin.

Hilda found that the last Jewish Trust Corporation office closed in Germany during 1962, and that claims administration moved to London. Details of settled cases were stored in Hamburg until the mid-1970s, when they were transferred to the Central Archives of the History of Jewish People in Jerusalem. The London office closed in 1980, and likewise moved its files to Jerusalem.

The Jewish Restitution Successor Organization experienced a similar history, although its Berlin and Frankfurt offices were kept open until during the 1970s. Like the Jewish Trust Corporation, its administrative files were shipped to the Central Archives in Jerusalem. While the Jewish Restitution Successor Organization acted on behalf of the Jewish Trust Corporation in West Berlin, the latter retained responsibility for all important decisions. It was unclear, therefore, under which group the family documents might be filed.

Contact was made with the Central Archives in Jerusalem. The representative cautioned that although the Archives held administrative files from both organizations, they contained only a random selection of case histories. After checking its records, the representative reported nothing could be found connected with Hilda's family property.

John discovered the existence of the United States Supreme Restitution Court of Appeals which he confused with the Supreme Restitution Court of West Berlin. The former was the final court of appeal in the American sector of West Germany, excluding Berlin, whereas the latter presided over restitution appeals from all three Western Allied zones in West Berlin. It started operating in October 1953 and closed five years later. John learned that Harvard University's Law School Library held online catalogues for some of the American Court of Appeals files. He contacted the reference desk and its people were helpful, but unfortunately, could not trace anything that matched Hilda's property address.

Meanwhile, Hilda discovered more family photographs in a second box in the garage. These photos painted a picture of contentment and affluence during the late 1920s and early 1930s. There were images of her mother playing as a child on congested lakeside beaches, visiting shipyards in Danzig (now Gdansk in Poland), photos taken of the family on ski slopes in Switzerland and France, and pictures of the spa town of Baden Baden. There was even a portrait of her mother, aunt, and Gertrud, the cousin her mother played with, taken when they were teenagers. Hilda fantasized about how her mother must have protected these treasures while she lived in Vienna, crossed the Asian continent by train, survived in Shanghai for six years, and eventually settled in San Francisco. In the same box there were travel documents and brochures her mother assembled following her visits to Berlin after the war. They were tied together like a batch of love letters, recalling a place that she had once loved.

Absent were scenes of Berlin adorned with red flags and Nazi symbols, of marching soldiers and civilian rallies, of S.A. "brown shirts," and members of the Young Girls League in their dark blue skirts, white shirts, black neckerchiefs, and ankle socks. If Hilda's mother had not been Jewish, at age fourteen, she could have joined this organization when Hitler came to power.

Soon, a compendium of papers accumulated on Hilda's kitchen table. As documents were translated, each was collated chronologically in readiness for the arrival of the materials from the Berlin State Archives. Several times Hilda reminded the Archives contact she was still waiting, and it wasn't until February 2018, six months later, that the final batch of papers arrived. Emails sent as follow-ups during October 2017 generated no replies, and phone calls ended up on a recording machine, with none of them returned. John recommended Hilda send a formal reminder with a copy addressed to the Central Services Office and the Office of the German Chancellor. His work in Human Resources taught him that employee discipline complaints, copied to the firm's Chief Executive Officer, or to the Governor of California, or to the Federal Bureau of Investigation and the White House, usually generated immediate attention and a prompt reply.

The idea worked, and almost instantly Hilda heard back from her contact in the Archives. The woman had been on leave but now had returned and would send the materials as soon as possible. Nearly three months later, the information arrived. Answers to Hilda's questions were beginning to emerge. If the parts could be put together, and combined with an understanding of legal and social conditions during the 1930s and 1950s, Hilda believed the mystery of her family home would be solved. Increasingly, she was optimistic the circumstances of the 1936 sale could be revealed, and she would know how the West German authorities dealt with her family's restitution claim during the early 1950s. It was going to take time to translate the large number of documents, but she anticipated the pieces would fit together.

The Central Archives in Jerusalem had not finished offering help. It wrote again, suggesting that Hilda contact the Berlin State Archives, but was told she already was in touch. It also referred her to two other organizations it thought might be able to help. One was the Federal Compensation Office (Bundeszentralkartei) in Dusseldorf, and the other the Regional Compensation Office (Landesentschadigungsamt) in Berlin. Both were contacted. Dusseldorf wrote back to state that while it administered the German Federal Compensation Act, any financial records concerning Hilda's mother would be held by the Regional Office in Berlin.

At first, the Berlin office was reluctant to disclose information, but eventually it provided summaries of monies paid to Hilda's mother after the claim for property restitution had been dealt with. Suddenly, Hilda found herself in possession of an abundance of information, requiring thorough translation and careful interpretation. Her family's story began to take shape, as Google Translate converted German text into English words.

11

Guardianship Court ("Pflegschaftsgericht")

ILDA FIRST INVESTIGATED the background to the 1936 sale and the circumstances that led to it. She integrated extracts from the garage correspondence with memories from her mother, and merged them with what she had so far discovered from the Berlin State Archives materials and the internet. The events sometimes made her feel cheerful but often aroused sadness or indignation.

As she examined family photographs, she imagined Berlin before the rule of Hitler as a vibrant, busy city, not beautiful, but crowded with the activities of people. Pedestrians would be seen everywhere, rushing to and from work, visiting museums, galleries, and universities, and shopping. Older folks would be resting on park benches watching the world go by, while children arrived at school carrying their satchel-style book bags (schulranzen) in readiness for lessons. In the evening, bars, cafes, and restaurants took over. All methods of transport were seen on the wide avenues and broad streets, everything from cyclists, horses and carts, to motorcycles, rickety trams, delivery vans, and recently assembled Opel and Daimler-Benz automobiles. Alongside the vehicles were newspaper stands, fruit carts, and stalls that sold trinkets and things. Behind these stood classical buildings, tall apartment blocks, large houses, and the occasional monument. But tragedy would soon arrive.

The family's misfortunes began during December 1929 when Hilda's grandfather suffered a heart attack and passed away a few days later. Hilda's mother was just eleven and her sister seventeen. Their mother was thirty-nine. The family lived in the largest apartment in the property they owned, comprised of a dining area, drawing room, four bedrooms, a game room, piano space, study, two bathrooms, and a bedroom used by the cook. The building's other twenty or so apartments were leased as homes to middle-class families, and the complex consisted of two buildings linked together. One fronted the main street and the other overlooked a side road that ran perpendicular. A row of six shops occupied the ground floor, and consisted of a fabric store, shoemaker, cleaners, florist, bookseller, and chemist. The building's caretaker lived in a small apartment in the basement.

On this particular afternoon when their father became ill, both sisters were home. The youngest was sliding down the hallway banister, and the sister-in-charge looked on scornfully. They were called upstairs to hear that their father had been taken seriously ill and was under care in hospital. Shortly thereafter, at age fifty, he passed away. He was a tall, good-looking man, who enjoyed horseback riding, ice skating, and swimming. His first loyalty was to Germany, and the second to his Jewish ancestry. During the First World War, he fought with the German cavalry on the Eastern Front and returned to Berlin in late 1917, as Russia negotiated peace with Germany following the Bolshevik revolution. Wartime service probably explained why his two daughters were born six and a half years apart. The year following his return, his parents-in-law gifted him the building in which he and his wife lived. He loved his family and enjoyed hosting tenants, neighbors, and friends for dinners and social gatherings.

After he died, control of the business passed to his wife. She grieved his passing, but as the pain lessened, settled into her new role as landlord. She was at ease with the tenants, used a bookkeeper to take care of financial matters, enjoyed meeting people, and pleased tradesmen by paying their bills on time. People trusted her. She was honest, deliberate, organized, and efficient. Simultaneously, she cared for her children and kept them in school.

Financially, the family was comfortably well off. A life insurance policy on her husband had paid a death benefit of 18,000 Reichsmark (U.S. $4,500), and there were considerable securities under management with a local investment firm. Additionally, a large amount of cash was kept in the home for contingencies and to cover anticipated expenses. According to what Hilda's mother said, there was more cash in the house than in the bank.

The family employed a large household, shopped at up-scale department stores, and imported high-end carpets for the apartments from New York. Both daughters received generous gifts and wore fashionable attire. Hilda's mother talked about visits to the department store, Grunfeld's, where she would drink pink lemonade out of a marble fountain in the basement of the outlet.

The eldest daughter was approaching the age of consent and developing into a beautiful woman. She was the source of pride for everyone in the family. There was no intention of restricting her career to the business; her mother wished her to live an independent life. She met a Polish Jew, eight years her senior, who worked as a book salesman in Berlin. They fell in love and married. He moved into the apartment and their first child, a daughter, was born in mid-September 1933. Records found by Hilda showed the payment of a dowry, a customary settlement for a Jewish bride at the time, but there was no documentation of the amount. However, it was likely to be substantial in recognition of the family's importance in the community. Her mother liked the son-in-law who helped manage the apartments and was given power-of-attorney to execute decisions affecting the building.

Nationally, during the early 1930s, the Weimar Republic experienced formidable economic challenges because of the worldwide recession that began with the Wall Street crash during October 1929. The German economy stagnated, unemployment soared, the value of the Reichsmark collapsed, and countries would not agree to a moratorium on First World War reparations. Simultaneously, one of the German government's most significant accomplishments was the establishment of gender equality. No longer were women considered merely housewives and mothers. They were encouraged to join the workforce and by 1930, a third of German workers were women. But attitudes were changing.

As unemployment rose from eight percent during 1929 to nearly thirty-three percent by early 1932, opinions started to shift and women were blamed for the country's low economic growth and increase in poverty. With more and more males unemployed, the idea of excluding women from the workforce gained support as a way of addressing mass unemployment. The National Socialists adopted the slogan: "children, church, kitchen" (kinder, kirche, kuche). Hitler announced that, if elected, he would remove eight hundred thousand women from the workplace.

There was also the German financial crisis of July 1931, when the banking system virtually collapsed. Depositors panicked as anxious crowds waited in line to withdraw money. Large banks closed. Hilda imagined her grandmother standing among these crowds, choosing to convert what little money she had in the bank into cash. She even wondered if her grandmother maintained a bank account.

During this time, renting the apartments became more difficult, but since most tenants were Jewish and professionals, they stayed in employment. Hilda's family experienced relatively minor consequences. Laughter and the screams of children persisted in the courtyard, and the local community held together to support each other. The neighborhood was home to a disproportionate number of wealthy business owners. Stores on the ground floor suffered a slight decline in revenue, but none were forced to close. Documentation found by Hilda reported that her grandmother received a monthly net income of around 1,200 Reichsmark (U.S. $250).

But conditions rapidly deteriorated once the National Socialists took power and Adolf Hitler became German Chancellor on January 31, 1933. The first serious repercussions occurred during April that year, following the March 23, 1933 Enabling Act that gave Hitler dictatorial powers. Difficulties began with a national boycott of Jewish businesses but worsened on April 7, 1933 when a law was passed that restricted Civil Service employment to people of Aryan descent. Jewish teachers, professors, judges, and Jews in other professional and clerical appointments under government control lost their jobs. They were fired. A similar law was passed shortly thereafter affecting lawyers, doctors, musicians, and notaries.

Consequences for the family business were serious and almost instant. Several residents lost their jobs, some decided to move, a few non-Jews left their Jewish-owned apartments, and one tenant simply disappeared. The hallways became quiet as families departed. Conversations between tenants focused on acts of violence witnessed in the streets, including Nazi-organized marches and demonstrations, and the boycotting of Jewish businesses. They discussed various ways to stay safe.

Increasingly, the lives of tenants were disrupted. For example, there was the unemployed newspaper editor who suddenly disappeared. He was last seen in a nearby café being arrested while other customers looked away. Another tenant, a lawyer, was forbidden to give counsel to non-Jewish clients and in a little over a year, he went out of business. A long-time resident, who was a pediatric doctor, had her name stricken off the German Society for Pediatrics and found her private practice picketed by two uniformed young men. She challenged them. They told her their instructions were to stand in front of her office and turn away all patients. Eventually they went away.

Up on the fourth floor lived a retired schoolteacher. She was dismissed from her job and given a small pension. She stayed to herself, relied on her son to bring rations, and avoided anything that suggested she was Jewish. She lived secretly in her apartment, even after it was sold, and managed to outlast the war. She was one of about seventeen hundred Jews in Berlin who survived. Survivors overcame betrayal, arrest, surrendering, death, and perishing in air raids.

As resident turnover increased, finding replacements became more difficult. The large size and multiple-room configurations of many of the apartments made them unattractive and prohibitively expensive for renters without children. At the same time, shops on the ground floor attracted vandalism, anti-Semitic graffiti, and street protests. Hilda's grandmother was confronted by formidable challenges in an environment that had become one of discrimination, intimidation, fear, and persecution. From a privileged and protected upbringing, she had been thrust into managing a business, economically threatened by the hatred of others. She realized the need to lease to individuals, not families. Kitchens and bathrooms had to be reconfigured and new equipment, plumbing, and lighting installed. Bedrooms were remodeled so that multiple tenants could live in the same apartment and privacy arrangements made for new residents. All of this was expensive. In addition, the heating system for the building needed improvements and the sewer lines and hot water circulation systems had to be upgraded. The roof began to leak, damaging ceilings on the fourth floor, and involving even more expense.

Financial reports sent to the local Tax Office in late 1934 showed Hilda's grandmother was leasing fifteen of the twenty apartments in the building. Two were vacant and three had been converted into commercial use. Two large apartments were in the process of being subdivided into five rentable units, and three of the occupied units were lived-in by multiple tenants. Five of the six shops still operated, but the bookstore had been forced to close. Annual rental receipts for the property were 36,500 Reichsmark (U.S. $15,000), but profitability was shrinking as revenues declined and unplanned expenses were caused by remodeling. At the same time, the price of utilities such as coal, water, and electricity, and the cost of taxes and insurance continued to rise.

A number of craftsmen demanded payment before they would start work and others increased their prices for Jews. An Aryan plumber, installing a new heating system for several apartments, required fees to be paid in advance and then performed poorly. Legal action could not be taken to recover his charges since it was too dangerous for a Jew to sue an Aryan. Another plumber was hired and a second invoice paid.

Among the garage correspondence, Hilda stumbled on references to two very surprising developments. The first caused her to return to the Land Register deeds. There was no mention in the 1933 document of a mortgage, but apparently one was taken out around the time the inheritance was registered. The existence of the mortgage explained why the 1936 transaction referred to a loan having been transferred to the buyer. For whatever reason, an interest-only loan of 90,000 Reichsmark (U.S. $36,000) had been granted by a life insurance firm during November 1933. The conditions were payment of a six percent interest charge, increasing to eight percent if payments fell into arrears, repairing plaster damage on the inner courtyard façade within six months, and taking out two life insurance policies, one in the amount of 20,000 Reichsmark (U.S. $4,800) to cover Hilda's mother's life, and the other of 10,000 Reichsmark (U.S. $2,400) to protect the life of the son-in-law. Mention was made that the loan was disbursed to the family on November 23, 1933.

The Berlin-based firm was the Friedrich Wilhelm Life Insurance Corporation, a large insurer and one of Germany's oldest. It had been established in 1866 and became a subsidiary of the Gerling Financial Group in 1922. Hilda assumed her grandmother chose the company because of its reputation and its willingness to loan a substantial amount. Presumably securing the mortgage required the family to document the ownership changes, even though the inheritance had occurred nearly four years earlier.

The second event was probably caused by the first, and might not have been anticipated by Hilda's grandmother when she took out the loan. The District Court learned that the two daughters each owned three-eighths of the property, and the youngest child was a minor, under age 21, and without a father. It immediately placed Ellen in legal protection under the supervision of a Guardianship Court. The Court judge appointed a legal representative to take custody of Ellen from December 4, 1933, and to be accountable for all of her property and financial interests, her health and welfare, and legal and official matters. Because she had lost her father, there was a risk that her wellbeing might be endangered, and she was unable to protect herself. Important decisions affecting Ellen's circumstances had to be brought before the judge and submitted to the Court for approval. Ellen's own mother could not be assigned this role because of her gender. Discussions and decisions were recorded by the Guardianship Court and filed under what were called "acts of care." Everything that affected the financial interests of this underage daughter had to be reported to and approved by the Court. Ellen's mother was responsible for requesting approvals and was levied a fee for the service.

Documentation showed the Guardianship Court hearings occurred frequently and Hilda's grandmother was always required to attend. Usually she was alone, but sometimes accompanied by her son-in-law. Failure to appear could lead to arrest. Hilda thought the meetings must have been frightening, managed by a Nazi-approved judge who was appointed to enable accomplishment of Nazi goals rather than look after a teenage girl.

Everything Hilda so far discovered made her want to find out more about what caused the property sale.

12

Planning for Exodus

THERE WAS NOTHING translated so far that showed the Guardianship Court was more concerned with the welfare of Hilda's mother than supporting National Socialism. Its actions and decisions appeared focused on interfering with the economic condition of the property rather than safeguarding the asset on behalf of Ellen. There were no signs of support for the family. It was all interference. Hilda and John could not determine if decisions taken were to protect the family business or as part of a plan to seize the family property.

Hilda knew the German Courts expelled Jewish judges during 1933, and those now practicing were either members of the Nazi Party or at least sympathetic to Nazi ideology. They were there to support Hitler's policies and were generally complicit in enforcing discrimination and persecution under National Socialism. Failure to act in support of Nazism would impede their rise in the judicial system. It was within the jurisdiction of these courts that, later, handicapped people were identified and murdered or sterilized under Nazi orders. It was easy to imagine that the Court had, as its first priority, the goal of confiscating Jewish assets. This could more easily be achieved if the life of a teenager could be threatened to secure cooperation and obedience from those who loved her.

Hilda asked John to continue the translation while she turned her attention to studying life in Berlin during the early years of Hitler's leadership and how these conditions could have affected her family. During this time, Berlin was a city of tensions. There was increasing hostility towards the Jewish community. Organized boycotts, designed to destroy or acquire Jewish businesses, occurred frequently. It was impossible to know what might happen next. Acts of vandalism and physical abuse were routine. At the nearby Kurfurstendamm shopping center, Jewish trading licenses were revoked and police closed the stores. The Charlottenburg Sports Club banned Jewish members. Ellen's cousin, Gertrud, was required to give up playing competitive tennis, a sport she had begun at school.

Streets were adorned with Nazi banners and insignia, German military personnel regularly marched in goose-step to the cheers of the crowds, Nazi salutes were enforced by the courts, and fascist gangs sought out Jews to attack. Public calm was over. Only the trams, trains, and steam engines seemed unaffected by this hostility. Some Jewish business owners affiliated with non-Jewish partners in an attempt to protect themselves, but most tried to remain inconspicuous to make a living, and hoped for better times to return. During 1933, the first concentration camp in Germany was opened.

One of the earliest anti-Semitic campaigns was the burning of books, or what was called literary cleansing. This occurred on May 10, 1933 when large numbers of "un-German" publications were publicly burned. University students organized the demonstrations and thousands attended. Afterwards, bookstores carrying Jewish authors could expect to be vandalized. Branes Bookstore, in the family building, purged itself of offensive literature but then watched as its business failed. The Jewish-owned cleaners and shoemaker also struggled through Nazi intimidation but were strong enough to stay in business until the property was sold. The family publishing company was ruined.

Residents of the building constantly suffered harassment from the police. Early on, it was the Sturmabteilung "brown-shirts" (SA) who came inside, randomly searching the apartments and businesses, and interrogating occupants. The situation worsened when the

Schutzstaffel "black-shirts" (SS) took control to enforce Nazi racial policies. They stopped and searched citizens at random and were much more brutal in their treatment. The regular police were forbidden to interfere. Finally, inhabitants had to contend with the Gestapo, or political police, whose actions were exempt from the law and who used spies and informants to target their victims.

Turnover occurred among the renters, with some who could not fully pay their leases asking to stay with a reduced rent. There was a doctor, dismissed by the Berlin Health Department, who exchanged his services for a waiver on a portion of his lease. Hilda's impression was that her grandmother went out of her way to protect people who might otherwise become homeless and would receive "protective custody" which meant they would be transferred to a concentration camp.

Jewish institutional support was available but not very effective. An organization was formed during September 1933 in Charlottenburg to assist with trauma resulting from Nazi persecution. However, this was a male-run organization and Hilda's grandmother found herself ignored. She asked the organization to petition the District Court to have her daughter's guardianship rescinded, but it declined to do so.

Hilda now understood the reason why the German Consulate insisted that the District Courts would hold financial records. The information was not kept in the Land Register but elsewhere in the judiciary. Hilda wasn't sure where all the information might be found but it seemed the Charlottenburg Guardianship Court held financial records connected with her mother and grandmother, and another source was the local tax office.

Once more, she wrote to her friend in the Charlottenburg Land Register, inquiring about the guardianship process and asking whether or not the "acts of care" from the Guardianship Court might be available. She received an answer during late December 2017. Her friend explained the purpose of guardianship was to protect the interests of minors and give them the rights of self-determination. This way they were protected against friends and relatives who might take advantage of them. She told Hilda records of meetings might still exist, but Hilda would have to contact another organization, the Supervision Court (Betreuungsgericht). This department had taken over responsibility for the function, and an address was given with a list of information the department would need to search its files. Hilda decided to wait and not to act on the invitation.

John was successful in finding out more about the Guardianship Court meetings. The Berlin State Archives were his source. Brief summaries of some of the meetings had been documented in legal papers and recounted how Hilda's grandmother typically would request the Court to authorize the borrowing of funds to cover the costs of remodeling, repair, and maintenance of the property. Sometimes approval was given and sometimes it wasn't. Several requests originated between early 1934 and the first quarter of 1936. One was approved in early 1934 for 4,000 Reichsmark (U.S. $1,500) to pay craftsmen invoices, and a year later, another line of credit was authorized for 12,000 Reichsmark (U.S. $4,500) to cover expenses associated with the apartment conversions and to settle overdue property taxes. The original request had been for 15,000 Reichsmark (U.S. $5,750), but the Court claimed it heard part of the credit was to settle a dowry debt with the son-in-law. The Court rejected the proposal on the basis it was unacceptable for an underage child to provide funds for her brother-in-law. A lower amount was belatedly agreed, and in late 1935, a request for an additional loan was turned down.

A requirement at some of these meetings was for Hilda's grandmother to sign sworn statements that usually addressed some aspect of the family's finances. Included were affidavits that acknowledged the apartments were her only source of income, her daughter, Ellen, had no assets other than the part-ownership in the building, the family's net monthly rental income never exceeded 700 Reichsmark (U.S. $275), the value of life insurance when her husband died was 4,000 Reichsmark (U.S. $1,500), and the property did not generate any net income during 1934 and 1935. The purpose of these statements was never explained.

Hilda could imagine her grandmother not being totally honest under these conditions and trying to keep private as much about her wealth as she could. The more that was revealed, the more likely family assets would be seized. By cooperating with the Court, she hoped her family might be left alone and her daughter would be safe.

It seemed by mid-1935 the family was finding it increasingly difficult to live off of the declining rental income. There was ongoing turnover among residents, shopkeepers experienced increased difficulties paying the rent, utility prices continued to rise, and damage from anti-Semitic behavior had to be repaired and paid for. Threatening phone calls began after the Nuremberg Race Laws were passed during September 1935. Hilda's grandmother was instructed to sell the business or face confiscation. Phone calls were always from men and anonymous. They warned of drastic Party measures if she did not sell quickly, and although initially she ignored the phone messages, they eventually became intimidating and very demanding.

Hilda's grandmother also tried to preserve the financial welfare of the family by stopping the life insurance payments. The Friedrich Wilhelm firm reacted angrily, issuing an order in late November 1935, demanding immediate payment, and taking legal action as soon as it realized the premiums would not be paid. The correspondence indicated the company lost its case and shortly thereafter notified the family it was recalling the mortgage, effective March 31, 1936. If repayment was not received, foreclosure proceedings would begin immediately.

It was impossible for Hilda's grandmother to repay the loan. She asked the Guardianship Court to authorize another mortgage, but it refused, claiming it was not in the interests of the underage child. The threatening phone calls continued and, reluctantly, Hilda's grandmother instructed her son-in-law to find a buyer.

While she waited, she began to consider what the family might do next once its source of income was lost. Emigration to the United States was high on the list. A sister who lived in New York cautioned her that obtaining a visa would take a long time, and German Jews were not always welcome in America. Canada was no better, since it required refugees to fulfill certain skill and wealth requirements. Even so, Hilda's grandmother believed leaving Germany was necessary and achievable now, because her youngest daughter could no longer continue her education and the son-in-law's business in Berlin had been destroyed.

John, at this stage, was close to completing the translation of all the Berlin State Archives papers, although it was taking longer than expected because of the length and complexity of some of the documents and the difficulty in interpreting many of the legal terms. New facts emerged continually, including early signs that a claim for restitution had been submitted during the early 1950s. Hilda and John decided they would work first on the details of the 1936 sale and then turn their attention to restitution.

13

The Sale

CONFIRMATION THAT THE son-in-law took charge of the sales negotiations at the beginning of 1936 was found in the correspondence between Hilda's mother and her sibling in London. Apparently, the son-in-law received requests to purchase the property during the prior year, but his mother-in-law repeatedly rejected all offers. She preferred to ask the Guardianship Court to authorize a new mortgage, but it persisted in rejecting the request because of its responsibility to protect the interests of the underage child. Instead, on March 6, 1936, the Guardianship Court judge gave permission for the family business to be sold, a decision that seemed contrary to the well-being of the seventeen year old ward-of-court.

The son-in-law used a Jewish broker to identify potential buyers and was advised by the architect who had assisted the family with the remodeling of the apartments. It was the architect who found the purchaser. Data on the condition of the building were provided, and negotiations were completed by the architect and son-in-law during late March 1936.

The Guardianship Court continued to refuse to approve a new loan, insisting it didn't want the underage child indemnifying potential lenders against possible losses. Special insurance was needed and this was expensive. Hilda and John wondered why the

Court didn't intervene with the Friedrich Wilhelm Life Insurance Corporation and ask it to delay the cancellation of the mortgage until alternative financing was found. Apparently, it was content to watch the lender penalize the family for its loss of two life insurance policies, and there was no evidence the life insurance firm imposed this same requirement on the new owner. The Guardianship Court seemed to act as if it was conspiring with the mortgage company to confiscate the property.

The "acts of care" recorded that the Guardianship Court established an approved asking price for the property of 214,000 Reichsmark (U.S. $86,500), using the October 1934 rental income report. The amount was equal to the property's annual income multiplied by a factor of six, a standard formula used to establish property prices in Berlin at that time. Details of the negotiations were not documented but concluded with the acceptance of an offer of 208,000 Reichsmark (U.S. $84,000). The judge was told the lower price was justified by the structural condition of the property and approved the sale. The transaction closed on April 15, 1936, when the Friedrich Wilhelm Corporation documented the loan transfer to the purchaser, and the local tax office recorded the change in ownership.

The Land Register recorded the sale date as March 31, 1936, and registered the approved price as 208,000 Reichsmark (U.S. $84,000). This was the same amount Hilda had seen on the document sent by her friend in the Land Register. Why the building was described "abandoned" in the transaction remained unclear. Maybe it was because the family abandoned the mortgage, or due to the condition of the building, or possibly the heirs abandoned the right to own the property. Whatever the reason, it was apparent that Hilda's family gave up the property at this time but were allowed to live in their apartment for a further eighteen months.

Correspondence written by Hilda's mother during the early 1950s indicated she believed the family stayed in the apartment because they feared the sales proceeds would be confiscated if they left their home and Germany sooner. It was also possible, since the transaction was just before the Berlin Olympics, that the authorities did not want the visibility of another displaced family.

Nothing in the correspondence explained why the financing was structured in the way summarized in the Deed of Ownership. The transfer of the Friedrich Wilhelm mortgage was obvious, but the division between an immediate payment and a deferred amount was irreconcilable with the family intentions of emigrating. There was a comment in one of the legal documents that the sellers might have been forced to accept the five-year deferral to enable them to complete the transaction before foreclosure proceedings would have begun April 1, 1936.

Apparently, once the sale was completed, the relationship between the buyer and Hilda's family became argumentative. The acquirer proceeded to use the legal system to pursue additional discriminatory objectives. The first action was when the Court allowed him to deduct 3,000 Reichsmark (U.S. $1,200) from the initial payment of 78,000 Reichsmark (U.S. $31,500), when it was released in mid-May. He claimed the repayment to compensate for overdue property taxes he had to pay and because the family received some of the April 1936 rents.

The relationship worsened dramatically during late 1936 when the architect, who was now working for the buyer, listed repairs that were considered necessary to complete before the purchaser could remodel the apartments. Total costs amounted to 24,000 Reichsmark (U.S. $9,700). The Guardianship Court sympathized with the acquirer, and despite Hilda's grandmother's rejection of the request, allowed the buyer to go to court where he successfully obtained a refund because the family was too afraid to object.

There were also indications that additional amounts may have been recovered. There was a note from the Berlin State Archives indicating the local tax office assessed an inheritance tax on the property of 27,000 Reichsmark (U.S. $11,000). There was no record that the Guardianship Court anticipated these additional expenses when it approved the sale, and they appeared not to be in the best interests of the ward-of-court.

Nothing so far had been found among the paperwork that explained what happened to the deferred payment.

The family relationships with the Guardianship Court continued to deteriorate. Hilda's grandmother planned a visit to relatives in Brazil and wanted Ellen to accompany her. The judge refused and instead placed the now eighteen-year-old under foster care, with a full-time guardian. It was agreed she could live with her sister and brother-in-law so long as the guardian was allowed free access to the home.

Hilda's grandmother began to examine countries that the family might relocate to following the sale. During the mid-1930s, there was very little global sympathy towards accepting Jewish refugees, and many countries limited the numbers because of fear of overpopulation, unemployment, and possibly the provocation of anti-Semitism. Britain required immigrants to demonstrate they had a job and funds on which to live. The United States process took too long, and Palestine had almost closed its borders. Controls in Palestine were in place to give priority to people who brought in capital, were young Zionists, or who had relatives already residing in Palestine. Central and South American countries were the most promising. Brazil and Argentina were accepting large numbers of displaced persons, and Hilda's grandmother had relatives living in Sao Paulo; she would visit them.

Before she could leave, she had to pay the Reich Flight Tax. This was a fee established in 1931 by the Weimar Republic to control the flight of capital from Germany during the banking crisis. Now the National Socialists were using it to confiscate Jewish assets from departing residents. To leave Germany, a tax clearance certificate was required, and regulations late in 1936 imposed a nearly eighty percent tax rate on declared assets. Hilda's grandmother complained her trip was a visit only, and she was not relocating, but this distinction didn't matter. Exactly how much she paid was not recorded.

Hilda discovered another letter among the garage correspondence, showing a German attorney tried unsuccessfully to recover the tax on behalf of Hilda's mother during the early 1950s. He wrote to inform her that the District Court lost evidence of the payment and therefore would not consider a reimbursement.

The trip to Brazil was by steamship, and the journey took three weeks. The Brazilian Consulate offered Hilda's grandmother and family refugee status but only on condition they convert to Christianity. This requirement, and Hilda's grandmother's dislike of Sao Paulo, prompted her to reject the invitation. Grandmother returned to Berlin in time to attend the birth of her eldest daughter's second child during August 1937.

Back home, the family's New York relatives mentioned an acquaintance in Vienna who they said would welcome the family and take care of them. Hitler had not yet invaded Austria, and the relocation appeared attractive. It would be safer for her youngest daughter, and her son-in-law could start-up a new business. Hilda's mother and grandmother were the first to leave. To avoid paying Reich Flight Tax, they traveled through Czechoslovakia and entered Austria from that country, and not from Germany. The Guardianship Court was not informed. The son-in-law's family joined them a few days later but, unfortunately, on March 12, 1938, Hitler and his Nazi troops invaded Austria to annex the country (what was called "Anschluss"). The harassment and persecution of Jews now extended to Vienna. Hilda shuddered when she remembered the stories her mother would tell her about living in that city.

Now it was time for Hilda and John to turn their attention to restitution and the actions her mother, along with her sister, took after the war. Multiple references were found in the correspondence, but the challenge was fitting the pieces together to create a coherent story. The litigation process was described in detail among documents sent by the Berlin State Archives. It was important to understand the events of the early 1950s and see if the information added clarity to the 1936 sale.

Seventeen years passed since the family sold the property, and the description of a restitution process was emerging. From the start, it was clear the 1936 purchaser objected strongly to the demands of Hilda's family and argued they were not forced to sell him the property. Throughout the documentation, Hilda's mother and aunt were placed at significant disadvantages. Their parents were dead, family records were lost during National Socialism, memories and hearsay might not convince the Courts, tenants from the 1930s were no longer traceable, and the two families did not have the financial resources to pursue lengthy and expensive litigation. By contrast, the purchaser was still able to receive income from the property, could readily solicit witnesses because he lived in Berlin, had the support of the finance companies, probably could gain access to the Guardianship Court records, and likely would receive sympathy from the German restitution judges. Another certainty recorded in the files was that none of the Guardianship Court judges involved with Ellen's underage care were alive to explain their decisions during the 1930s, and there was no one available at the life insurance company willing to testify the true reasons for recalling the mortgage.

Hilda and John realized before they progressed much further, it was important to understand how the West German restitution process worked and in what way the judges were expected to conduct themselves. Some of what they read was confusing, and an appreciation of the law seemed necessary if they were to understand the outcome of the claim. Fortunately, they had two attorney friends, Donna and Steve, visiting them from New York in a few days' time, and they would ask for their guidance.

Donna and Steve were close friends. They had first met several years earlier during a vacation in Italy, and ever since had maintained a close friendship. Indeed, thereafter, they enjoyed several vacations together. Steve was retired from a high-level legal position in the Bronx and his wife taught law at a nearby university. The four of them would have ample time to discuss Hilda and John's questions as they toured the Northern California coast. If their friends didn't have answers, hopefully they would direct Hilda and John to where explanations could be found.

The prospect of solving the mystery of Guntzelstrasse 44 was increasing, although the couple became apprehensive when correspondence indicated the legal system might not be very sympathetic towards Hilda's family. Further examination of the Berlin State Archives documents was necessary.

14

Friends from New York

HILDA WAS DELIGHTED when she discovered her mother was one of the first Jewish refugees to seek property restitution in Berlin. Legal papers showed recovery to be Ellen's primary motive, not compensation. The purchaser would be reimbursed for its return if Ellen was instructed to do so by the courts. It was Ellen's home, and she wanted it back. Her sister in London had been told about her intentions, but not until after the process began. Hilda thought this was discourteous until she read in court papers from the Berlin State Archives that her grandmother wanted her youngest daughter to inherit the entire property.

It was late 1952 when Hilda's mother appointed an attorney in Berlin to represent her interests. There was no explanation about who the person was, and Hilda speculated he must be an acquaintance of the family from before the war. Letters were exchanged and a claim quickly prepared. Then the first unanticipated problem emerged. A separate demand had already been filed by the Jewish Trust Corporation on behalf of the missing heirs. After some dialogue, Hilda's mother agreed to consolidate her legal action with the institutional litigation, and her Berlin attorney accepted the role of observer. The lawsuit was filed with the Charlottenburg Restitution Chamber on September 17, 1953. Restitution Chambers were established at the District Court level, with a panel of three judges, the requirement to conduct public hearings, and instructions to publish their findings in writing.

During September 1953, the first federal West German law guiding the restitution process was approved. These regulations were regarded by some as poorly drafted, lacking in clarity, and not providing sufficient administrative advice to support uniform implementation of the law. Additionally, prejudice existed among the Chamber judges due to their loyalties towards former National Socialist colleagues.

Many sectors of West Germany had not fully accepted responsibility for the nation's treatment of Jews before and during the war. Hilda found a study published a few weeks prior to the submission of her mother's claim. It showed that among the people surveyed, only five percent felt guilt towards the Jewish population, and nearly a quarter thought Jews were responsible for what happened. Another thirty percent thought the country should provide some form of restitution, but the remainder believed Germany owed them nothing. Hilda suspected the defendant belonged to the latter group, given his adamant opposition to restitution and his interpretation of the new regulations. He used legal terms unfamiliar to Hilda and John, and these would be discussed with Donna and Steve after their arrival from New York.

Hilda and John's preliminary assessment of the relationship between the two sides was it was acrimonious and the litigation probably would be lengthy. The defendant opposed any form of settlement, writing to Hilda's uncle in England that he would resist all efforts to secure restitution. He declared there was no persecution of Jews when he bought the property, that it was sold voluntarily, that he paid a fair price, and the seller received the proceeds from the sale. His hostile attitude was aggravated during April 1954 when the Trustees for the Military Government in Germany took title to the property. He appointed an attorney to develop his defense and to seek out witnesses to testify in his support. Several were traced, the most important being the architect involved in the 1936 sale.

Documents published by the Restitution Chamber named two co-defendants. The first was a representative from the Friedrich

Wilhelm life insurance firm, and the other a spokesperson for a home loan credit company that granted a line of credit to the defendant in late 1951. The amount had been 19,500 Deutsche Marks (U.S. $4,650), and apparently was to cover the cost of rehabilitating the apartments from damage caused during the war. There was a third loan, in the amount of 51,800 Reichsmark (U.S. $20,000), that had been approved during February 1942. This turned out to be made by the same life insurance company that granted the initial mortgage and curiously was approved about the same time as payment of the five-year deferred mortgage fell due.

Hilda imagined what her mother's opponents might have looked like. First, there was the accused who was a rather serious and unremarkable, selfish and short-tempered person, subject to a range of illnesses. It was the latter that kept him away from combat during the war. In fact, there was a letter from his doctor to the Restitution Chamber asking the judges to be considerate of the defendant's health, because he suffered from traumatic epilepsy and a severe form of cardiac disorder that if triggered, would have life-threatening consequences. The doctor included in his letter the statement, "the patient's life expectancy is likely to be very short." However, what the defendant lacked in physical strength, he made up in mental determination, and with the aid of an experienced and talented attorney, the litigation was heated and acrimonious.

The attorney was a portrait of the classic German, a man over six feet tall, endowed with a mass of blonde hair, who stared through piercing blue eyes, and dressed smartly. He loved adversarial situations and thrived on shrewdness to harass his opponents. He was detail-oriented, using information as a weapon against his antagonists.

The architect was the other person Hilda visualized as she began to realize the important role he played in the Restitution Chamber's hearings. He was a short, squat, and almost bald man, apparently in his sixties, who peered through shifty green eyes. He spoke furtively, hoping to say whatever his audience wished to hear.

On the plaintiffs' side, there was only the institutional attorney who was physically present. He held a strong moral conviction that his clients had been cheated out of ownership. He argued according to the rules, using technical knowledge rather than a detailed understanding of the family's circumstances. He was a tall, thin, bespectacled American of German-Jewish descent.

And finally, there was Hilda's mother and aunt who possessed neither the funds nor the desire to return to Berlin. Most people they knew before the war had disappeared and they believed they would be unsafe if they went back to Germany. All they possessed were memories of what their mother had told them. Each hired a local attorney to give advice and to liaise with the Jewish Restitution Successor Organization. Neither of them understood the details of the West German legal process but trusted their attorneys did.

It was the legal principles that were the foundation of the restitution process that Hilda and John wanted to understand. There were concepts such as rebuttable presumptions, linked relationships, and something called "venire contra factum proprium" (good faith and fair dealing). What these terms meant was unclear, and how they might affect the outcome of the lawsuit uncertain. Hopefully, their friends from New York would help.

The Jewish Restitution Successor Organization had written a critical letter to the Restitution Chamber registering objections over the use of some of these principles. It argued, that if applied, West Germany would continue to persecute the Jewish population and legalize the confiscation of property that occurred before and during the war.

At the start of January 2018, in a restaurant near Monterey, California, Hilda and John began their conversation with Donna and Steve. Donna did most of the explaining, and Steve occasionally interrupted to add his agreement to what Donna was saying.

"Rebuttable presumption, that's easy," replied Donna, after John explained the difficulties he and Hilda were encountering. "It's an assumption legally taken to be the truth unless someone can prove otherwise. But in what context is it being used here?" she asked.

Hilda tried to explain. "Because my family is Jewish and the confiscation took place between September 14, 1935 and May 8,

1945, the property ought to qualify automatically for restitution. The first date is the passing of the Nuremberg Laws, and the May date is Germany's surrender at the end of the war. However, from what we have read, the judges are able to declare the sale legitimate if the sale price was reasonable and my family received the proceeds. I'm not exactly sure what this means."

Donna resumed her explanation. "It means the defendant can rebut the assumption of discrimination if he demonstrates the property was sold at a fair price and your family received the money. Fulfillment of these criteria makes the sale legal. If he does that, it's possible the judges might declare the sale would have occurred without National Socialism and reject the claim for restitution. However, it shouldn't be that simple and shouldn't be delegated to personal interpretations. Regulations supporting the law should define terms such as fair value, the appraisal methodology, a definition of 'receipt of proceeds', and how evidence from Nazi times should be used."

"Then why did the Jewish Restitution Successor Organization recommend something called 'juris et de jure?'" Hilda asked.

"That prevents the defendant from contradicting the assertion that the property was confiscated," Donna explained. Steve nodded his head in agreement. Donna continued, "It's an irrevocable presumption that binds the sale to National Socialism. It would guarantee restitution so long as your mother reimbursed the purchaser in accordance with court rules. It's the opposite of rebuttable presumption but rarely used today. An example is children under the age of seven who are incapable of committing a felony."

Hilda went on to explain, "It's clear to John and me that the property was purchased because of National Socialism. That's what my mother always said and it looks as if there may have been collusion between the Guardianship Court, the life insurance company, the buyer, and the architect."

"We also think a portion of the sales proceeds was never received," added John.

"A significant amount from the initial payment seems to have been recovered and we assume the five-year deferred installment was never paid. The tax authorities also claimed a substantial amount. The main concern is how the Guardianship Court 'acts of care' will be used and how they might influence the Restitution judges."

"Also, one final question," John added. "There's something called 'venire contra factum proprium' in the correspondence. It's Latin, we know, but we are not sure what it means in this situation."

Steve answered, "Translated it means that once a written testimony has been submitted to a Court, it cannot be contradicted. A witness who disputes a prior sworn statement may be considered in violation of good faith and fair dealing. It forces the Courts to decide which version is correct and they don't like having to do that. Typically, they take the side of the first declaration. But hopefully this situation doesn't affect your mother?"

"I hope not, but we are not sure," added Hilda.

With that, Donna and Steve were thanked for their guidance, and all four returned to eating. The conversation shifted to contemporary family matters.

A little later, Hilda spoke to her friend Marjorie, a labor attorney who lived nearby. Marjorie agreed with what Hilda had been told, in so far as she understood civil law, but warned that the law defines justice, not the other way around. Hilda shouldn't be surprised if she discovered proceedings that seem to her to be unfair.

It was now time to resume researching the documents.

15

Reconstructing Events

I T WAS EARLY March 2018, and the papers from the Berlin State Archives had been translated and chronologically collated with the family correspondence found in the garage. It had proven a time-consuming task. Anticipation arose whenever something new was discovered. The documents dated from the 1930s and 1950s and were prepared using manual typewriters. Mistakes were crossed out and individual letters occasionally illegible, presumably because the typewriter key was not hit hard enough. With some documents, the type-face faded or the paper discolored.

The worst was finding German terms that did not have an English equivalent or sometimes were old enough to no longer exist in modern-day German. There were also expressions with multiple translations. The challenge was to select the correct one.

Fortunately, several lengthy documents were the same as those found in Hilda's garage and therefore had already been transcribed into English. Probably the most interesting piece of information was that the Guardianship Court "acts of care" were missing when the restitution process began. Hilda and John slowly reconstructed past events and started to understand what happened.

The first legal deposition was submitted to the Restitution Chamber by the defense counsel at the beginning of March 1954. In his affidavit, the defendant dismissed the claim for restitution as unjustified, made no counter-offer, and asserted there had been no discrimination or persecution of Jews in Germany at the time of the sale. He expounded that anti-Semitism only began in Germany during April 1938 when Jews were required to register their property.

The testimony claimed the purchase price of 208,000 Reichsmark (U.S. $84,000) was generous since the local tax office valued the property a year earlier at 183,400 Reichsmark (U.S. $74,000). Investigating on the internet, John confirmed the tax office used a very arbitrary and subjective set of appraisal criteria that might even have lowered the value knowing the property was owned by Jews and occupied by them. The Guardianship Court appraisal was more objective, using actual rental income multiplied by a market factor reflecting economic conditions at the time. However, it overlooked the impact of vacant or under-utilized apartments that had become a significant phenomenon during the period of Jewish persecution

In addition, the defendant's attorney referred to the poor condition of the property and claimed it was infested with rats. Invoices for the cost of exterminating the rodents and completing essential repair work were currently unavailable, but the defendant's architect was contacting tradesmen to see if copies could be found.

The sale had not been forced. The transaction had happened because the eldest daughter was in dispute with her mother over money needed by the son-in-law to start a new business. Reference was made to the architect who could testify that the son-in-law had been looking for a buyer since early-1935.

It was also claimed that the proceeds from the sale were fully disbursed. The defendant took over the outstanding Friedrich Wilhelm mortgage and paid the 78,000 Reichsmark (U.S. $31,500). The District Court forwarded the payment to the seller during mid-May 1936. The promissory note guaranteeing payment of the deferred 40,000 Reichsmark (U.S. $16,000) was registered with the District Court and retrieved by the son-in-law during January 1937. He supposedly sold the note to a private banker a few weeks later, who in turn sold it to a customer. The deposition confirmed the defendant paid the interest due on the deferred amount and cancelled the debt on November 21, 1942.

This was a major surprise for Hilda and John. Previously, they assumed the payment was never made, and the arrangement was a device for the purchaser to avoid paying some of the sale price. Now they knew what really happened. Exactly how much the son-in-law obtained for the note was not recorded, but it was likely to be less than face value. It also was probable the proceeds were needed to cover living expenses for the family if most of the first installment was recovered by the courts. Converting the note to cash was an indication the family had decided to emigrate, and they did not want to leave assets behind in Berlin. Anything left would likely be confiscated.

The attorney declared that if the defendant was forced to return the property, he would expect reimbursement of the original purchase price, assumption by the clients of the three outstanding loans, compensation for all property taxes paid during the ownership period, reimbursement of expenses for building improvements and necessary repairs after the war, and an amount equal to a five percent annual interest rate since date of purchase computed on his client's initial investment.

Specific information was provided listing the building improvements. The buyer converted several large apartments into smaller ones during late 1936 and 1937 in order to return the business to profitability. These changes were similar to the ones made by Hilda's grandmother in 1934. The defendant also provided information on rental income received during the period 1938 to 1942, showing annual receipts averaging 40,700 Reichsmark (U.S. $16,300). The defendant's architect would provide details of these improvements if more information was needed.

The Jewish Restitution Successor Organization quickly submitted an opposing statement, challenging the entirety of the defendant's declaration. It alleged the purchase price of 208,000 Reichsmark (U.S. $84,000) was unacceptably low and supported the assertion by providing its own appraisal. The assistance of a construction expert was used to place a 1936 value on the property of 314,000 Reichsmark (U.S. $126,500). The construction expert adopted a valuation method based on comparable sales but because few could be found, supplemented the calculation using estimated net income and a capitalization rate. The Jewish Restitution Successor Organization argued this method was more accurate than the Guardianship Court process.

Whether the sellers were free to use the sales proceeds, the Jewish Restitution Successor Organization did not know but claimed it was clear the sale took place due to National Socialism. Allegations that the property was in a bad state of repair were rejected and the assertion the building was infested with rodents denied. Restitution was justified and the plaintiffs agreed to compensate the defendant in accordance with Court requirements.

The Berlin attorney who Hilda's mother had originally employed had spoken with the Jewish Restitution Successor Organization and as a result, wrote to the San Francisco attorney helping Hilda's mother, warning him that the defendant was trying to rebut the presumption of confiscation. He asked the San Francisco colleague to have his client prepare an affidavit as soon as possible and submit it to the Restitution Chamber.

Meanwhile, the two sisters exchanged correspondence about the progress of their claim. Hilda's aunt had been trying to contact the Berlin attorney to discuss what she was supposed to do. Both found the process confusing and unnecessarily complex, and they encouraged each other to do things that would take their minds off the conflict. Hilda's father was in the process of launching a printing business in San Francisco, Hilda's mother was happy looking after her three-year-old daughter, and both parents had recently become United States citizens. Hilda's aunt and uncle in London were recuperating from arranging their eldest daughter's wedding, and their recently established leather goods business was prospering.

The next legal exchange took place during June 1954. The defendant's attorney announced he now had proof of the reasonableness of the actual purchase price. He had found documentation in the

District Court showing details of the family's annual revenues for each apartment and store during late 1934. If a multiplier of six was used, the market value of the property would be 213,000 Reichsmark (U.S. $86,000). The actual price paid was slightly lower but justified by the poor condition of the property. The attorney had also been told that 1936 leases in Berlin were ten to fifteen percent lower than during the prior year. Thus, if anything, the price paid by his client was generous. He rejected the valuation method proposed by the Jewish Restitution Successor Organization.

The most serious and worrisome development for Hilda and John was that the attorney located the Guardianship Court "acts of care." They were in Vienna. Apparently, they had been sent there on September 19, 1938. The authorities presumably learned of Ellen's whereabouts after the invasion of Austria and forwarded the files to the local police department for enforcement.

Hilda remembered her mother talking about a visit from the authorities in Vienna to tell her that once she reached age twenty-one, she would either have to leave Austria or would be deported to a concentration camp. It was for this reason, a few days after her twenty-first birthday, she married her Austrian fiancée.

The defendant's attorney told the Restitution Chamber that the Charlottenburg District Court had helped him find the "acts of care," and after reviewing them, he returned them to the District Court for safekeeping. He found the records extremely informative. They gave proof that the purchase price was fair, that the sale was legally approved, that the sellers agreed the offer, that the building was in a state of disrepair at the time of sale, and most importantly, the owners were subject to serious financial difficulties unrelated to anti-Semitism. During the months before the sale, it had been necessary for the Guardianship Court to approve loans so that the family could pay tradesmen bills, renovate several apartments, and settle tax debts. There was no mention in these "acts of care" of any discrimination and persecution.

Evidence that the property was in poor condition was given to the judges. The architect prepared an itemized list of repairs that were necessary at the time of the sale. However, when Hilda and John inspected the inventory, it appeared most items were related to property improvements rather than essential maintenance. Included were refurbishing the courtyard, replacing stoves, sinks and bath tubs, repairing and repainting the street front, replacing corroded radiators, and stripping and re-wallpapering several apartments.

The architect offered additional testimony, claiming the son-in-law told him the family needed to complete the sale by April 1, 1936 to avoid foreclosure proceedings. Otherwise, the property would be taken away from them. The second deposition concluded with the statement, "The guardianship reports give clear insight into the family's financial problems, and there is no mention of persecution."

Not surprisingly, the Jewish Restitution Successor Organization strongly challenged the evidence, and in particular, the availability of the Guardianship Court "acts of care." These were unreliable, the attorney claimed. They came from a Court that was part of the Nazi persecution apparatus used to confiscate Jewish property. The records should not have been released in the first place without the approval of his clients. They were personal and private. He went on to challenge the legitimacy of Austria releasing the information to another country and concluded, if the Restitution Chamber is going to admit them, "I need a copy for review."

The defendant's counsel countered he had acted lawfully, that mutual assistance procedures existed between Austria and the Western Sector of Berlin, and the files had been returned to the District Court for safekeeping. He would request their release again if the Restitution Chamber judges wished to study them.

Meanwhile, the judges were under pressure to set a hearing date. Co-defendants Friedrich Wilhelm and the other finance company were alarmed by the delay, and in mid-August, the Chamber announced a meeting arranged for October 6, 1954, starting at 10.00 am.

At the same time, the Jewish Restitution Successor Organization repeated its objections to the release of the guardianship reports, but to no avail. The attorney at the Jewish Restitution Successor

Organization attorney also criticized the Guardianship Court's decision in March 1936 not to approve a mortgage for the family and instead, force a sale. There was no good reason to withhold consent, he argued.

He also condemned the defendant's assertion that no persecution of Jews took place before April 26, 1938. He listed fifty-five anti-Semitic regulations approved under National Socialism between the date of the sale and the end of March 1938. A statement from Hilda's mother, prepared during January 1953 for her original attorney, was also presented. It referenced the legal action taken by the purchaser against the family several months after the sale to recover a large repayment. None of these arguments seemed to influence the judges. They appeared to focus on events up to the date of sale and not concern themselves with anything that happened thereafter.

The defendant submitted another deposition, this time listing more data from the Guardianship Court "acts of care." He claimed these proved the dire financial conditions of the family. They were why the Court withheld approval of a replacement mortgage. Whatever loan that could have been approved would not have been sufficient to overcome the family's financial problems

The Restitution Chamber's first public hearing was now only two days away, and neither Hilda's mother nor aunt would attend for reasons of cost and personal safety. They would rely on the advocacy of the attorney working for the Jewish Restitution Successor Organization. Hilda eagerly looked forward to finding out what happened as she and John continued to put together the story from the Court documents they had been sent.

16

October 6th, 1954

I T WAS A chilly Wednesday morning, with a grey, overcast sky
scattering occasional showers on the streets below, as attendees
entered the imposing and dignified Court House to participate
in the restitution hearing. Their mood was somber and serious. No
one wanted to be there except possibly the attorney from the Jewish
Restitution Successor Organization. The defendant felt, like many
Germans, that it was shameful to be ordered to give up property
and to admit guilt for something that occurred almost twenty years
previously, over which he had no control. Today it was Germans who
were suffering, not those who claimed persecution under National
Socialism many years earlier. He was the victim of an unwelcome law
imposed on West Germany by victorious Allies.

The mood among the three judges was no better. Their role was to
impose unwanted regulations on fellow citizens and show sympathy
towards people they did not consider casualties of war. It was an
unsatisfying responsibility to condemn the work of their predecessors
who operated under Nazi rule. At least they no longer wore the
symbols of Nazi allegiance on their judicial gowns or underneath
their uniforms, and the requirement to give and receive the "Heil
Hitler" salute had ended.

The judges took their seats, looking across the windowless room
towards the defendant, his attorney, representatives of the two

financial institutions, and the lawyer from the Jewish Restitution Successor Organization. Behind these participants sat members of the accused's family, several potential witnesses for the defendant, including the architect, the Berlin lawyer known to Hilda's mother, and a number of observers.

The presiding judge opened the hearing by explaining the purpose of the Restitution Chamber. He began, "It's responsible for adjudicating return-of-property claims when the parties affected cannot reach an amicable out-of-court settlement. The law makes whole those who lost property illegally because of National Socialism. This Chamber's duty is to investigate the claim made by the Jewish Restitution Successor Organization and reach a conclusion based on consistent and objective standards of evidence."

He thanked both sides for attending and acknowledged receipt of written testimonies, but he proceeded to express concern that nothing had been received from the applicants. Their attorney was ordered to obtain signed affidavits from Hilda's mother, and separately from her sister and husband, by mid-November. The judiciary did not dispute the petitioners were Jewish and eligible to file a claim but questioned whether the family lost their land because of National Socialism or for some other reason. There appeared to have been a legal sale and the defendant had informed the Chamber that he fulfilled its conditions.

The attorney accepted the request but cautioned the justices. "The court must understand my clients were forced to leave Germany many years ago, and fortunately found countries willing to welcome them. Today they live overseas, have families to take care of, and do not have the funds to participate in these hearings."

The bench acknowledged the situation and then switched its focus to ask the defendant why he rejected the restitution claim. He replied, "The accusations are unjustified. I legally purchased the property at the request of the owners who were in serious financial difficulties at the time. They couldn't make their business profitable, they were late in paying their tradesmen for services provided, and repeatedly needed loans to cover expenses. None of these circumstances had anything to do with National Socialism. "

"What evidence do you have that justifies your claim?" asked one of the judges.

"We have obtained Guardianship Court records from the 1930s, thanks to the efforts of my attorney, which show the seriousness of the claimants' financial circumstances. They began well before the arrival of National Socialism. They started when the head of household died during December 1929, and as early as November 1933, the heirs to the property needed to take out a large mortgage to support their business. They requested several additional loans during the following eighteen months. We have copies of signed testimonies from the plaintiffs' mother that confirm the details of these problems and make no mention of anti-Semitism. They were filed with the Guardianship Court records."

The presiding judge looked to the Jewish Restitution Successor Organization's attorney for a response. "We strongly disagree with this portrayal. The family was well-off following the death of the husband, and the 1933 loan was used to settle family financial matters and enable the owners to fund the cost of converting several large apartments into smaller ones. Jewish families were leaving Berlin during this period because of National Socialism and were being replaced by couples and single tenants. It's false to claim these events had nothing to do with the political situation at the time. The family chose not to use its own resources because of political uncertainty."

The attorney continued, "The owners never wanted to sell. They were forced into the sale when the mortgage company, Friedrich Wilhelm Life Insurance, withdrew its loan, and the Guardianship Court refused to do anything about the situation, including approving alternative credit. These obstacles, along with threatening phone calls the family was receiving, made it financially impossible and physically dangerous to retain ownership of the building. You don't expect Jewish people to acknowledge these political reasons to a Court responsible for imposing Nazi regulations, do you?

"It's our reason for opposing the use of the Guardianship Court 'acts of care.' That Court supported the interests of National Socialism, not the welfare of children. It's ludicrous to believe the family was going to disclose personal wealth to the judges. Persecuted Jews at the time limited their conversations to what they thought would satisfy the authorities. We strongly believe the Chamber should not base its decision on records from a Nazi organization. It cannot know if the information is truthful, and there is nobody alive from those meetings who can testify to the truth of what took place."

"Those are strong allegations," interrupted the judge. "We don't see any evidence to support your opinions. While the defendant provides clear written testimony, we have nothing from your clients to counter his declarations."

Redirecting attention to the defendant, the senior judge asked, "Can you explain what you paid for the property and why you believe it was a fair price?"

The defendant hid his irritation caused by the attitude of the plaintiffs' attorney and answered, "First, it was up to the seller to choose the buyer. The owners could have chosen someone else, but I think I was preferred because of having the funds to pay cash, I was willing to let the family stay in the apartment indefinitely, and they had a need to dispose of the building by the end of March. The 208,000 Reichsmark (U.S. $84,000) sale price was negotiated with the seller's son-in-law, and the Guardianship Court approved the amount as reasonable. The Court proposed a slightly higher figure, but my architect justified the lower value based on the condition of the property."

He continued, "I assumed the outstanding mortgage, immediately paid the family a large cash amount, and fulfilled my obligations under the deferred credit arrangement. I don't see what else I could have done. If you doubt the condition of the property, you should talk to the architect who will explain the work necessary before the building could be made financially successful."

The Jewish Restitution Successor Organization's attorney was asked for his reaction. He said, "Again, we strongly disagree. Our surveyor places the market value of the property at 314,000 Reichsmark (U.S. $126,500) and we want the property returned. We will fulfill our responsibility to compensate the defendant in accordance with legal requirements."

"Did your clients' family receive the proceeds from the sale?" asked one of the associate judges.

"We're not sure. The daughter-under-care at the time says her mother was sued to recover a part of the purchase price because of the condition of the property, so we can assume that at least something was paid."

The defendant was asked to comment. "An amount of 78,000 Reichsmark (U.S. $31,500) was paid during May 1936, less a small amount that was deducted from the lump sum because I became responsible for some of the taxes owed by the family and the sellers collected part of the April rents. Obligations for the deferred mortgage were fulfilled, including the interest payments. I distributed the principal amount in 1942. I know the son-in-law traded my promissory note to a private banker in early 1937, although that decision had nothing to do with me. Much of this can be verified by the architect if you want to ask him."

It was apparent to the onlookers that progress to achieve a settlement was not going to be easy. Both sides were unwilling to concede any argument or offer a compromise.

The judges decided to call the architect to the witness stand. He stood in front of the panel trying to look confident, despite his nervousness. Every so often, he would look across at the defendant for reassurance and encouragement. He smiled slightly and hesitated when asked difficult questions.

"First, were you ever a member of the National Socialist Party or associated with it?" asked the presiding judge.

"No, I never was and politically always tried to stay neutral. However, I did work closely with credit organizations and sympathized with their need to recover loans from Jews who were abandoning the country. "

"And how did you become involved in this sale?"

"The son-in-law asked me to help. He first talked about selling the property during early 1935, but nothing happened. I don't think his mother-in-law was ready to sell, although her son-in-law often talked about disposing of the building to have the funds to start a new business. A year later, the financial situation of the family and condition of the property had significantly worsened, and she changed her mind. A broker friend guided me through the sale process and I persuaded the defendant to purchase the building during March 1936. I told him about the property's condition and he asked me to negotiate on his behalf. The son-in-law wanted the transaction completed before the end of March and offered me a completion bonus if I could achieve that."

"What did you think of the mother-in-law when she decided to sell?"

"I told her it wasn't a good decision. I cautioned her over the sale."

"And did you ever hear about the threatening phone calls the family claims they received about the same time?"

"No, never."

The panel of judges thanked the architect and asked him to return to his seat.

The Jewish Restitution Successor Organization's attorney reacted to what he had heard by telling the bench he believed the architect was untruthful. His testimony should not be trusted and there was a conflict of interest since he now was in the paid employment of the defendant. The plaintiffs would testify to a very different picture. There had been no efforts to sell the property during 1935. The mother was always opposed to the idea, and this was the first time he had heard that the architect criticized the family for selling.

Since there was nothing else to discuss, the presiding judge adjourned the meeting. He said he would accept the Guardianship Court "acts of care" as evidence, but he made no mention of the possibility that the Guardianship Court was part of the persecution process and its records might misrepresent what actually took place. The judge addressed the importance of hearing from the plaintiffs as quickly as possible. As soon as their affidavits were received, the parties would be given an opportunity to review the content, and if they chose, could reject the need for a second hearing. No one present seemed particularly pleased with the conclusions of the meeting.

17

Intense Reactions

THE ATTORNEY FROM the Jewish Restitution Successor Organization left the court house, concerned the judges had already decided to favor the defendant who had provided credible argument that the property was bought and paid for legally. However, the defendant's testimony was spiteful. He argued that the sale was solely due to the family's financial mismanagement. Clearly some of the repairs and needs for remodeling were the direct consequence of National Socialism. It was shocking to hear the judges accept the statement that there had been no persecution of Jews before April 1938. Hilda and John found it hard to believe the mistake was accidental. The attorney seemed determined to correct this falsehood.

It was equally shocking that the Restitution Chamber would allow the "acts of care" to be entered as part of the evidence. They were obtained by threatening the life of a teenage girl, their truthfulness could not be determined, and they gave an important advantage to the accused because they could not easily be challenged. There was no one alive to confirm their accuracy, and the plaintiffs could only use hearsay and memory to support their allegations.

A few days after the hearing, Hilda's mother received a letter from the attorney relaying his anxieties about the claim and stressing the need for her affidavit to clearly demonstrate that political pressure caused the 1936 sale, not financial difficulties. She must persuade the judges that her mother never wanted to sell the property and only disposed of it because of coercion. The testimony was required by the Restitution Chamber no later than November 11, 1954.

The attorney had told the Restitution Chamber that another loan should have been approved in 1936 to avoid the sale, but the judges disagreed with him. They referred to a statement recorded by the Guardianship Court that this borrowing was too expensive. This was because of indemnity insurance needed to protect the interests of the underage girl. Also, he was searching for witnesses who were acquainted with the property in the mid-1930s, but he was not optimistic about success. He had found a doctor who lived in one of the apartments before the war, but the doctor declined to testify because he did not wish to take sides publicly.

Hilda's mother was angry and upset. The defendant was disputing the truth about what really happened and using false information obtained from the Guardianship Court. The "acts of care" should not have been made available in the first place and were being used to tell lies. She wasn't sure how to fulfill the needs of the attorney because she was only a teenager at the time and did not fully understand what was happening. She drafted her ideas and mailed them to her relatives in London, asking for comments.

She proposed to state the family sold the property because of a Nazi ultimatum and not because of financial difficulties. She would insist the apartments were kept in good condition, despite Guardianship Court statements to the contrary, and disagree with the 1934 affidavit that her mother received only 4,000 Reichsmark (U.S. $1,600) in death benefits.

Ellen would claim the sale took place because of the September 1935 Nuremberg laws that legalized discrimination against the Jews, and the sinister phone calls. Once the mortgage company threatened to cancel the loan, there was no alternative but to sell and extract as much wealth from the property as was possible.

Her relatives wrote back supporting the testimony. They would submit something similar and include additional specific information where possible. For example, they would mention the 18,000 Reichsmark (U.S. $7,500) life insurance payment their mother had spoken about and object to the use of the Guardianship Court "acts of care" amount. Even so, from what they had been told, they were not optimistic that their claim would be successful.

Because it was important for the sisters to review the depositions with their local attorneys before submitting them, preparation took longer than expected. The Restitution Chamber delayed the deadline for receipt until December 15, 1954.

The London relatives were annoyed by the Chamber's process and the deadlines that were difficult to meet. They also expressed alarm over the rising costs of their London lawyer. Unlike in the United States, contingency fees in the United Kingdom were prohibited.

In San Francisco, Hilda's mother wasn't sure what would happen but decided to be patient and delegate responsibility to the Jewish Restitution Successor Organization. She was enjoying a peaceful and happy life in San Francisco and loved everything American. Preparations were being made to send her daughter to Kindergarten at the Frank McCoppin Elementary School, and she and her husband had begun saving to buy their first home in the United States. It would be modest in comparison to the Berlin apartment building.

Around them, they watched San Francisco react to its new state of affairs. A few weeks earlier, during June 1954, Proposition E had passed to save half the San Francisco cable-car network from bankruptcy, and more recently, during November 1954, a 5,000,000 dollar bond had been approved to begin construction of Candlestick Park. She was also considering she might have to return to work once her daughter started school.

Six weeks after filing the plaintiffs' depositions, the defendant's attorney submitted further testimony challenging their content. He had completed a more thorough review of the Guardianship Court "acts of care" and was certain they convincingly contradicted all that had been said by his adversaries. There was overwhelming evidence that the family encountered continuous and severe financial difficulties, including arrears in property taxes, unpaid craftsmen invoices, a failure to pay life insurance premiums, the need for additional loans, and tax declarations signed by the deceased grandmother that she received no property income during the months before the sale. How could his opponents claim that the family received substantial earnings when this was contrary to their mother's statement? They were either misinformed or lying. He repeated that none of the "acts of care" mentioned National Socialism, and the architect remained available to corroborate the poor condition of the property at the time of sale.

The defendant also asked that the testimony from Hilda's mother be dismissed. She was underage at the time of the sale and ignored German law when she ran away to Austria. Her statements could not be trusted.

The consequence of these exchanges was furious disagreement between the two sides. Hilda's mother forcefully rejected the defendant's submission, accusing him of being a Nazi and a proponent of the "Final Solution." She was outraged that the architect supported the defendant, arguing his actions were for money, and his motives were anti-Semitic. She was appalled that the words of a German Aryan would be trusted over those of a Jewish widow.

The defendant continued to use the "acts of care" to oppose restitution. Hilda and John were coping with many unanswered questions as they studied the documents. Why did the Guardianship Court fail to intervene with the Friedrich Wilhelm firm to have it defer the cancellation of the mortgage? Why was only six weeks' notice given before foreclosure proceedings would begin? Why did the defendant purchase the property if it was in disrepair and unprofitable? Who made the threatening phone calls, and why? And what was the role of the architect who switched sides once the sales negotiations were complete?

None of the plaintiffs' recollections appeared to have impressed the judges. They could not provide paperwork to back up their statements. Witnesses could not be found to corroborate their stories, and even though the confiscation had to have been the result of National Socialism, the defendant persisted with his claim that anti-Semitism was not the cause of the sale.

In one final effort to weaken the defendant's defense, the Jewish Restitution Successor Organization supplied the Restitution Chamber with a list of eight anti-Semitic regulations implemented during the first quarter of 1936. It hoped they would demonstrate unequivocally that persecution of the Jews was taking place during the time the sale was negotiated. None of this information appeared to influence the opinions of the judges.

The decision to return the property now rested with the Restitution Chamber. During February 1955, the Chamber announced it would convene another hearing, scheduled for March 3, 1955. The date was later postponed to March 23, 1955 for reasons not explained. It might have been because the judges wanted the son-in-law to attend. He declined, not wishing to return to Berlin under circumstances that he considered dangerous. Strangely, on March 12, 1955, the Chamber launched a search of Berlin records to identify his former address and business activities during the early 1930s. There was no sign that anything was found.

Participants at the October 6, 1954 hearing were invited to this second meeting. The architect advised he would be present, and Ellen heard that her original attorney would attend as an observer. The attorneys from both sides would be in attendance, as well as representatives from the two co-defendant finance companies. Only the defendant would be absent. He was too ill to attend. The judges seemed close to reaching a decision.

18

An Answer

IT WAS A crisp, cold, dry morning as participants arrived at the court house to attend the second hearing at the Restitution Chamber, scheduled to begin at 9.00 am on March 23, 1955. Once inside, people were shedding their winter coats, hats, gloves, and scarves. Outside, the chilly northeast wind had stimulated their minds and now they struggled to stay alert as warmth in the building diminished their acuteness.

They had traveled through a city still recovering from the effects of the war. Burned-out buildings were commonplace and included such notable structures as the Reichstag and the Kaiser-Wilhelm Memorial Church. Elsewhere were bombed-out factories and damaged apartment buildings. The streets were nearly back to normal with the noise of public transport and private vehicles, and pedestrians once again characterized the sidewalks of Berlin. Stores were open, and cafes offered coffee and tea to passers-by. Parks had been reclaimed, and vacationers returned to the beaches at nearby lakes. Large numbers of refugees arrived daily from East Germany, and were given shelter in acceptance camps until processed and allowed to stay in West Germany. East German passport restrictions would not be tightened until December 1957, and the Wall would not be erected until August 13, 1961. Important to everyone was the news that the Western Allies would end their occupation in six weeks' time.

The defendant's attorney and architect were talking. The plan was for the architect to testify later in the morning detailing the shabby conditions of the apartments when the property was purchased, provide copies of invoices for roof repairs and restoration of heating, plumbing, and electrical installations necessary at that time, and submit a letter describing how the coalman had to sue the family to recover payment for delivery of fuel. The architect would also provide extracts from the "acts of care" to show how the family fell behind with its water supply payments and was late paying the Guardianship Court for its services. The obligation to compensate the Court for its supervision of the underage daughter was another surprise for Hilda and John. The architect would also confirm under oath that the family neglected essential maintenance during the years before the property was sold.

The Jewish Restitution Successor Organization's attorney and the lawyer that Hilda's mother used as an observer talked together. Their concern was the judges' acceptance of the Guardianship Court "acts of care" and the absence of witnesses to corroborate the alternative story provided by Ellen and her sister. Flaws in the restitution process could cause the judges to decide the sale occurred legally and thereby give the defendant the opportunity to rebut the presumption that the sale was due to Nazi persecution.

When the architect took the stand, the exchange with the plaintiffs' attorney once more became hostile. The attorney accused him of giving only his personal recollections and not technical information. Allegations were made that repairs carried out after the sale were caused by the defendant's decision to remodel the property and not because of essential maintenance requirements.

The presiding judge interrupted and asked the witness to return to his seat. He added it was unfortunate that the son-in-law was unavailable to give his side of events. The meeting adjourned after the Chamber announced it would publish the judges' findings as quickly as possible. Two days later, a sixteen-page report was distributed with the judges' decision summarized on the last page. The document provided a summary of the testimonies and an assessment of the evidence.

Hilda was surprised she had not found the report among the garage papers left by her mother. Obviously, it was very important. In fact, she had no correspondence dated after February 1955, until the arrival of materials from the Berlin State Archives.

The Restitution Chamber's findings opened with an overview, reminding readers that the hearings were to address the defendant's appeal against a restitution order, on the grounds he purchased the property legally, at a fair price, and that the seller received the proceeds from the transaction. The defendant alleged the sale was due to family debt and the condition of the property, and not because of National Socialism. Testimony from both parties had been obtained, and it was mentioned that the Guardianship Court "acts of care" had been important reference documents. Their content greatly influenced the results of the hearings. The findings praised the child custody procedures and stated they were "consistently administered by people with special expertise, who would be embarrassed if their knowledge was violated."

The judges were indifferent to the Guardianship Court being a Nazi-appointed organization that might have been complicit in seizing Jewish property. No reference was made to other motives that might influence the Guardianship Court, and there was no effort to seek out more information by speaking to people involved in the legal system during the early 1930s. This seemed to be a shocking shortcoming in the way the Chamber fulfilled its responsibilities, thought Hilda and John.

The affidavit submitted by Hilda's mother was not mentioned in the findings, presumably because the Chamber complied with the defendant's request and rejected her testimony. Worse still, there was mention that the statement from Hilda's aunt and uncle had been disregarded, because it conflicted with the architect's evidence. The comments in the findings were, "the architect is a deliberate and objective man who holds to the truth and says no more than he can really answer," whereas they regarded the plaintiff's evidence as "completely lacking in detail and not dependable for honesty." The judges' conclusions seemed to be very one-sided and gave Hilda and John no sense that justice was being dispensed.

Thereafter, more specific aspects of the property transaction were addressed, starting with the purchase price. Hilda remembered earlier correspondence from the attorney at the Jewish Restitution Successor Organization stating, in his experience, Restitution Chambers never agreed a sales price was below market value. Hilda's family circumstances were to be no exception. The judges once more used the Guardianship Court "acts of care" as proof that the transaction was legally authorized and the sale price was established using reliable appraisal methods. If anything, the judges thought the amount was very generous, considering the condition of the property.

The findings made no mention of the appraisal submitted by the Jewish Restitution Successor Organization of 314,000 Reichsmark (U.S. $126,500). It was simply ignored.

With respect to whether the funds were disbursed, the Chamber concluded the defendant had fulfilled his obligations. He paid the amounts that had been agreed upon, and it was up to the seller to decide how the funds should be used. There was no comment on the deferred payment. Similarly, no reference was made to the reimbursement amounts mentioned by the plaintiffs that were reclaimed by the buyer after the transaction closed. The judges focused on the sales transaction only and did not concern themselves with anything that happened after the sale was concluded.

It felt as if the Chamber was unwilling to confront the truth of what caused the sale. The judges relied on Guardianship Court records to identify financial mismanagement and the poor condition of the property as reasons for the sale. There was also comment on the so-called "maturing" of the mortgage, and the judges seemed to regard its cancellation as normal business practice. They believed the sale had nothing do with discrimination against Jews and concluded, "if these conditions had existed in a non-Nazi period, it is clear from the 'acts of care' that the property would have been put up for sale."

As a footnote, the judges recorded "considerable reservations" over whether or not the family received threatening phone calls. They also doubted that there was a large amount of cash in the house. If this was true, why didn't the family use some of it to pay off its short-term debts and avoid the sale?

The report concluded with the statement, "The defendant has provided grounds for rejecting restitution under the requirements of the law, so the claim of the applicants is rejected."

Hilda and John were appalled by what they had just read. It wasn't so much the outcome that annoyed them, but how the Restitution Chamber reached its decision. There seemed to be clear evidence the judges were predisposed to support the false honesty of their legal predecessors. They could not see that they were maintaining discrimination and continuing to persecute people who had survived the Holocaust. The fact that a teenage girl had been held hostage as part of this process was ignored.

It was difficult to know how Hilda's mother reacted to the outcome since there was no follow-up correspondence between her and her sister, or with the Jewish Restitution Successor Organization. Hilda could imagine her extreme disappointment and how likely it was that her mother gave up at this point. The signs were she accepted defeat and delegated the decision for any subsequent appeal to the Jewish Trust Corporation. Evidence for this interpretation was her mother returned to work that summer, after five years at home caring for her daughter. She found a job as a sales assistant in the five and dime store, known as Kress's, at Market and Fifth Streets in San Francisco. Hilda assumed there was nothing else her mother could do to seek reparations at that time. Presumably, she decided to wait for new German regulations that would broaden compensation rules to include a wider range of deprivations, such as death of the provider, loss of personal belongings, canceled career plans, and other freedoms impacted by National Socialism.

The saying of Hilda's mother was, "I suffered enough for all of us," but she never forgot the property. It was her "Heimat" in German, her emotional bond, the symbol of a happy childhood, a place of deep connections, the home of her parents, a place that she loved. It was her private dream, even after she settled into a happy life in America.

The reaction of the attorney at the Jewish Restitution Successor Organization was also missing from the paperwork. It was easy to imagine how irate he must have been as he witnessed the weaknesses in the law that he had identified as denying him success. It had been easy for the defendant to rebut the claim the sale was caused by National Socialism. By using the "acts of care" he demonstrated to the satisfaction of the Restitution Chamber that the sale was legally approved, that the sale price was fair and accepted by the sellers, and that the proceeds were made available to Hilda's family. These records were relied upon to show that financial mismanagement was the reason for the sale, not National Socialism. It didn't matter that the financial difficulties were a direct consequence of anti-Semitism.

Finally, it appeared that the affidavits submitted by Hilda's grandmother to the Guardianship Court during the 1930s had received precedent over Hilda's mother and her aunts' later testimonies. The earlier documents convinced the judges that the family was never well-off after the father died, earned very little from the property during the 1930s, received no other source of remuneration, and was never subject to racial discrimination. The rule of "venire contra factum proprium" prevailed in the minds of the restitution judges, notwithstanding the Nazi circumstances under which the Guardianship Court operated. The likelihood that signed statements were obtained under duress was high, and the reasoning existed that they should have been considered illegal and invalid. The judges disregarded this alternative and felt entitled to dismiss the more recent testimonies that contradicted what had previously been stated.

Across the North Sea, the Restitution Chamber's decision was received with disappointment by Hilda's aunt and uncle. They were now successful shopkeepers and took the decision as a sign to end their legal action. The cost of litigation was high and continuing the claim was made more difficult by the untimely illness of their English legal consultant, and his sudden death a little time later. Replacing him would be expensive and the likelihood of recovering the property improbable. As a result, they withdrew from the legal action.

But all was not lost. The Jewish Trust Corporation was not so easily persuaded to abandon the claim. It disputed the Restitution Chamber's reasoning and authorized the Jewish Restitution Successor Organization to submit an appeal.

Hilda and John had been dismayed by the findings of the Restitution Chamber. Maybe the couple misunderstood some of the German text in the report or mistranslated its words, but they didn't think so. It was easy to become angry, but there was not much they could do about the situation. Legal avenues had closed, according to the advice they had received earlier. Publishing a book might draw attention to the apparent injustice, but there didn't seem any point in fighting and arguing through the legal system. This had all happened a long time ago and the prize was uncovering the story.

Hilda asked John what he thought of the outcome. His answer was one word: "disgusting."

She spoke to friends about the idea of sharing her research and revelations with others. They agreed it was a good idea to publish a book. John volunteered to help once the fact-finding had been completed. There was still the need to examine the appeals process with the Civil Senate of the Berlin Court of Appeals. How did the Appeals Court respond? Maybe it adopted a different point of view to the request that Guntzelstrasse 44 be returned to its rightful owner?

19

The Appeal

HILDA AND JOHN examined the Berlin State Archives to see if additional testimony was submitted to the Court of Appeals before the hearing that took place on June 13, 1956. They found nothing. Neither the defendant nor Hilda's family had added more information, and there was no correspondence between the two Courts. Access to the case dossiers kept by the two Jewish advocacy agencies would have helped, but these were not available.

The one indication why the Court of Appeals was reviewing the claim was a reference in the judgement published six weeks after the June 13 meeting. The document mentioned an appeal lodged on April 10, 1955 by the Jewish Trust Corporation, because it believed the Restitution Chamber did not consider the prosperous lifestyle of the family and had not allowed sufficient time for the son-in-law to comment on the architect's testimony. Reacting to the petition, the defendant filed a motion demanding its dismissal and that costs be awarded against the plaintiffs. From the records it was unclear who attended the June 1956 hearing, but it seemed more symbolic than substantive.

The Court of Appeals answered the prosperous lifestyle allegations by stating the plaintiffs' recollections did not correspond to the actual course of events recorded in the Guardianship Court "acts of care." Once more, the functioning of a Nazi Court received priority over claims from those who had been mistreated. There was also comment that the architect's testimony was much more trustworthy than the declaration made by the son-in-law and his wife.

Otherwise, the Court of Appeals mostly repeated the same findings as the Restitution Chamber except for a few remarks suggesting it performed a small amount of its own research. For example, it referred to the Guardianship Court "acts of care" from March 11, 1935. Apparently, these included a letter signed by Hilda's grandmother that stated the underage daughter should become the sole inheritor of the property. The Court of Appeals linked this statement to the decision by the Guardianship Court not to approve a new loan, because it did not want the underage girl responsible for such a large debt.

The "acts of care" also revealed that the District Court recovered about 35,000 Reichsmark (U.S. $14,000) from the family after the sale to settle overdue property taxes, mortgage interest arrears, unpaid craftsmen invoices, essential repair work, and the finder's fee for the architect. This amount presumably was taken from the first installment of the purchase monies, making the need to convert the promissory note into cash much more urgent for the family. Another surprising fact was the local tax office, in April 1937, recorded cash assets held by Hilda's grandmother and youngest daughter at March 31, 1936, as high as 130,000 Reichsmark (U.S. $52,000). The amount supposedly included proceeds from the sale of Guntzelstrasse 44. Curiously, there was no analysis of why this amount should be reported when a month earlier, the Guardianship Court had listed family assets at only a few hundred Reichsmark. The Court of Appeals commented that the discrepancy might be explained by the family hiding cash at home in readiness for its departure from Germany. It did not occur to the Court of Appeals that this contradiction might also suggest the Guardianship Court information was not necessarily accurate and complete. Even more preposterous was the Court's speculation that the family agreed to a five-year deferred mortgage because it had no intention of leaving the country. To Hilda and John, these were evaluations full of contradictions and inconsistencies.

Another important observation was the threatening phone calls. The Court of Appeals concluded these were only the opinions of the plaintiffs and not necessarily true. Even if they did occur, they were not the cause of the sale. The Court also accepted that the market value of the property should be 183,400 Reichsmark (U.S. $74,000), which was the lowest of the three appraisals. It gave no reasons for its selection. The only comment it made was the defendant paid well above market price for the property, and it criticized the Restitution Chamber for not registering this discrepancy. The appraisal from the Jewish Restitution Successor Organization of 314,000 Reichsmark (U.S. $126,500) was acknowledged, but no reason was given for its rejection.

It didn't take Hilda and John long to anticipate the outcome of the Court of Appeals review. Little more was done than endorse the findings of the Restitution Chamber. The Court of Appeals declared it was unable to change the decision of the lower court unless it found facts demonstrating the Restitution Chamber misunderstood the case. There was no evidence of this.

Additionally, it was determined that no anti-Semitic behavior had taken place to influence the sale. The price paid was reasonable and the transaction legally approved by the Guardianship Court. The sellers received free disposal of the monies. The Court's decision was to uphold the defendant's motion but not to award him costs. The latter was not permitted by the regulations.

Hilda and John were in disbelief. All the Court of Appeals had done was to corroborate the decision of the Restitution Chamber without feeling compelled to seek out other evidence. Once more there was anger and disappointment, but Hilda would not allow emotions to control her outlook. Her motto was always to look on the bright side, and now, at the very least, she knew the answers to questions she created during her June 2016 visit to Berlin. She was saddened to think that her mother first was required to abandon her home "in" Berlin and eleven years later was abandoned "by" Berlin.

Hilda consoled herself with the knowledge that her mother's life in America was a happy one. She knew her grandmother would be proud of her daughter's accomplishments, and while it appeared ownership of the building was lost forever, the decisions of 1936 saved the lives of two women.

There remained the possibility that the Jewish Trust Corporation might appeal the decision to the highest court in Berlin, the Berlin Supreme Restitution Court. Here most judges would be non-German, but apparently the request was never filed. Hilda and John could find no correspondence to explain why this action was not taken. A note from the Berlin State Archives mentioned that the Supreme Restitution Court was informed of a potential claim, but one was not submitted. On November 9, 1956, the Supreme Court notified the Restitution Chamber that a request for review had not been received, and therefore the litigation was closed. It returned the case file to the Charlottenburg District Court, asking the Court to certify on the Land Register that the refund certificate, issued in April 1954 to the Restitution Trustees, had been cancelled. The property was now to be returned to the defendant.

Hilda believed she was at the end of her research. She had discovered so much, most of it unexpected, after a long and difficult investigation. The effort had been very worthwhile and she was pleased she now possessed a comprehensive understanding of what happened to her mother before and after the war. Her study had begun as an inquiry into a Berlin property once owned by her family and had transformed into revealing the practices of West German Restitution Chambers after the Second World War.

There was more information she could request to continue her investigations such as details from the "acts of care" and how the real estate company came to acquire the property. She might pursue these opportunities in the future, but for now, she was satisfied to take a sabbatical and record her recent experiences. The story would be a signal of shame for the West German legal system. Additionally, she was aware her mother received some compensation from West Germany after the restitution claim was rejected, and she wanted to find out why. Discovering this piece of information would be the ending of her adventure into the ancestry of her family.

20

Conclusions

IT SEEMED A long while since the project started in Berlin. Hilda
would never forget standing in front of her family's ancestral
home and letting her mind flood with memories of her mother.
Unlocking secrets behind the history of the building had been
invigorating and she was pleased that the fact-finding was more or less
over. The research itself was triumphant, even though the outcome
was disappointing, and the treatment of her family shocking.

She was amazed by the willingness of people to furnish information that helped with her investigations, especially those who lived
in Berlin. The store owners and occupant of the apartment were particularly noteworthy, as was the Rick Steves tour guide, and the wonderful woman in the Charlottenburg Land Register who diligently
produced the foundation for Hilda's fact-finding. She and John were
also indebted to the Berlin branch of the Federal Office for Central
Services (BADV), the Association of German Banks (Bundesverband
deutscher Banken), the State Archives of Berlin (Landesarchiv Berlin), and the Berlin Compensation Office (Landesentschadigungsamt). Outside Germany, important guidance came from the University of Jerusalem's Central Archives for the History of Jewish People,
the Harvard Law Library, and the Washington D.C. Simon-Skjodt
Center for the Prevention of Genocide.

Hilda appreciated the many friends who helped with translation

and offered advice along the way, and she would always be grateful
to her cousin in England for her unselfish collaboration, in spite of
it provoking memories of the treatment she suffered in the British
orphanage during the war. And there was John, the special friend, who
persuaded her to carry on when obstacles appeared insurmountable.
Somehow, he always uncovered new perspectives and took charge of
future action. Finally, there was Donna and Steve from New York,
who explained the basic principles of West German restitution law.

Hilda's admiration for her mother's tenaciousness to survive grew
enormously. It was easy to remember past events, but how much
more frightening it was to confront worsening anti-Semitism, not
knowing how it might next manifest itself. As for her grandmother,
Hilda could not find the words to describe the horrors and hazards
she experienced during struggles to take care of her two young
daughters. Hilda repeatedly needed to convince herself that the
unbelievable events she had just encountered had in fact taken place.

The most disgraceful discovery was the attitudes of West German
restitution judges. They used vague and poorly crafted regulations to
create more discrimination against the Jews and make them forego
owning their homes for a second time. It seemed the destruction of
the Jewish community in Germany had not ended just because the
Second World War was over. Holocaust denial flourished, and during
the mid-1930s, what better way to spy on three defenseless women
than forcing the youngest to be placed under the supervision of a
Guardianship Court? Hilda would never know her grandmother's
emotions as she attended those meetings, but she could imagine
the tenseness and stress of the conversations. By means of cross-
examination, the family's state of affairs and intentions were known
to the authorities and could be used at any time to persecute and
discriminate. National Socialism first sought to squeeze her family
out of the German economy and then out of the country. Restitution
Courts loyally accepted evidence created by Nazi sympathizers
and Nazi Party members, in preference to accepting the subjective
evidence of plaintiffs.

And there was the defendant in the restitution case who had died a half-century earlier. It was hard to grasp why he so forcibly argued anti-Semitism in Germany did not occur before April 1938. He seemed to be one of many Germans who tried hard to deny the truth once the war was over.

Hilda also recalled other organizations that helped with the research, such as the San Francisco German Consulate and several law firms. There were no plans to reconnect with these, although she imagined sending them copies of the book when it was published. She would do the same for the people who had helped in Berlin.

There was also the real estate company, Onnasch Baubetreuung GmbH and Co., which presumably was the present owner of at least part of the property. Hilda would inform the company in due course of what she had discovered. She wondered if the firm knew anything about the history of the building when it purchased it in the early 1990s. It was doubtful it would acknowledge her correspondence, but Hilda's satisfaction would be making it aware that she knew what took place.

She also had selfish thoughts about compensation. First and foremost, she dreamed of owning or having use of an apartment in Berlin to permit her and her family to reconnect with Germany. Occupying accommodation in her mother's childhood home would be a way of celebrating her mother's centennial on October 10, 2018. Hilda recognized the fantastical nature of her thoughts, but they persisted. What would her mother have done if she had repossessed the property in 1955? Life in Berlin was difficult, and both her mother and aunt were happy in their adopted countries. Neither likely wanted to return to Germany, but maybe they would have become absentee landlords.

The idea of annually celebrating the history of the building also surfaced. No one Hilda met during the June 2016 visit had known the property was once owned by a Jewish family. She read of the Denk Mal Am Ort ("think on the spot") that celebrates the lives of former Jewish residents of Berlin forced to leave their homes by the Nazis. Maybe Guntzelstrasse 44 could be added to that list.

There were other issues to consider, for example, the unreimbursed

Reich Flight Tax (Reichsfluchtsteuer). Possibly, the Berlin authorities could agree to investigate what might be done for people whose assets were stolen by the Nazis but where tax records were lost during the war. Hilda knew from the last few pages of the Berlin State Archives that the Berlin Compensation Office, during March 1963, borrowed the restitution files relating to her mother. This was presumably to examine her eligibility for a pension, and maybe the value of the Reich Flight Tax was factored into this calculation. Hilda did not know.

Her last delusional aspiration was the idea of thanking people who helped her along the way. Was it possible to show appreciation in the form of a charitable contribution to an organization of each person's choosing? Such an offer should include the shopkeepers, the occupant who showed Hilda the apartment, the lady at the Charlottenburg Land Register, and the Rick Steves travel guide. Maybe this was something the current owners of the building might consider.

A side effect of Hilda's research was to recall her childhood memories. She remembered the summer vacations in the Santa Cruz Mountains, the family moving into its own owned home, and her mother's pride when she purchased her first new car. Where had the funds come from? Some were earned, but a large contribution likely came from West Germany. What had her mother been paid, and for what? Who made the payments? Answers to these questions were the final pieces of the puzzle that Hilda wanted to complete.

First, she read about the compensation laws established by the West German government after the restitution regulations were introduced. A West German statute called the Federal Compensation Act was introduced in the summer of 1956 to compensate persons for various losses of freedom caused by National Socialism. This was known as the BEG-Gesetzestext. In July of the following year, the BRuG (Bundersruckerstattungsgesetz), or the General Act Regulating Compensation for War-Induced Losses, was enacted, providing compensation for a broader range of deprivations. Hilda read that in September 1965, West Germany passed the Final Federal Compensation Act that widened eligibility for BEG compensation. Payments were either in the form of an annuity or lump sums. Hilda was curious to know how well her mother had fared under these regulations.

The final pack of materials came from the Compensation Office in Berlin. Once more, Hilda realized her mother had been an early applicant for compensation. Nothing was paid before 1960, fifteen years after the War. In that year, her mother received a lump sum, compensating her for the loss of freedom while she was in the Shanghai Ghetto from May 1943 to May 1945. The start date coincided with Japan's establishment of a Jewish restricted ghetto in Shanghai, and the finishing date corresponded with Germany's surrender at the end of the war. The payment was equivalent to thirty-six United States dollars for each month of captivity.

Further lump sums were received from 1964 to 1973. The first two were for losses of personal belongings and the interruption of education. During January 1970, a third payment was made to compensate for physical and emotional exhaustion in Shanghai during the 1942 to 1947 period, and in 1974, she received by far the largest award. It was nearly 60,000 Deutsche Marks (U.S. $21,500), and compensated Hilda's mother for career impairment. It was equivalent to two years of average wages for an American at the time. The settlement covered a period of thirty years, from 1942 until November 1973, and thereafter, a regular monthly pension was paid for the rest of Ellen's life.

Hilda recalled her mother giving up employment in late 1974 and how she and her parent's lifestyle improved thereafter. Although her mother visited Berlin and Vienna on subsequent occasions, she always left her heart in San Francisco. Hilda imagined herself living in Germany, looking after a block of apartments, and speaking German, but in reality she preferred where she was in Novato, California.

Having completed her investigations, Hilda could now resume all aspects of her regular social life, lengthen the time committed to daily exercise, take greater care of her children and grandchildren, spend time refurbishing the home, and continue to travel to faraway places.

Her journey of discovery had been turbulent and unpredictable. She smiled as she thought about her mother choosing to invest in real estate during the last few years of her life. Maybe the profession was hereditary in the family. She knew by now why her mother sent her to etiquette school during the mid-1960s, why the Viennese were disliked so much by her mother, the reasons for her mother distrusting Germans, and Ellen's lifetime fondness for her cousin, Gertrud.

Hilda had taken charge of the sole survivor of her mother's real estate business, a rented detached house located in nearby Petaluma. This responsibility now took on a special meaning. Hilda realized how fortunate she was to have been born, thanks to the foresight of her grandmother who was willing to sacrifice everything to keep her two daughters safe from harm. What might finally result from Hilda's research, she didn't know, but what was important was that at long last, she knew about the remarkable war-time lives of her grandmother, aunt, and mother.

Postscript

HILDA AND I thank you for reading our story created by German National Socialism during the 1930s and the implementation of the West German legal system during the early 1950s. Eventually, the family in the narrative enjoyed contented lives in San Francisco and London. However, the journey to safety was long and brutal. Our story began with the disposal of a Berlin building, a very important building for the family, and ended with insights into the administration of the West German legal structure after the end of the Second World War.

There are places in the novella where we interpret what we have learned and express opinions about what happened in the situations we encountered, but in essence, every event in the book actually took place. This has been a story of what happened to a very well-off Jewish family living in Berlin at the start of the 1930s.

If you have time, you are welcome to post a review on Amazon, or any other site you might choose. If there are questions, you are welcome to ask them. Use my author website: johnrcammidge.com, and Hilda and I will try to answer.

Writing is a new career for me after working a life-time in Human Resources. I published *An Unplanned Encounter* several years ago under the author name of Jonathan R. Husband, and am currently writing a full length literary fiction titled *Bonfire Nights*. It focuses on life in Britain from 1965-1975. It's a love story combined with a business tale and an introduction to birdwatching.

Printed in Great Britain
by Amazon